# STEVE

*my path from pain to power and breakthrough living*

## KILLER

# GRACES

*navigating through life's
biggest challenges*

*with* MATTHEW HOSE

Killer Graces
*my path from pain to power and breakthrough living*
By Steve Melen, with Matthew Hose

ISBN: 978-1-7351657-1-4
Library of Congress Number 1-9063619341

Joint Venture Publishing
Blue Sky R&D, LLC

Printed in the United States of America

# DEDICATION

Dedicated to my daughter,
who helped me recover and
transform into a better version of myself.

# DISCLAIMER

Many names in this story have been changed to protect the identities of those involved. Much of this story takes place during a time when I was recovering from cancer, addicted to pain medication, or dependent on alcohol, so some events may be lightly fictionalized. However, the overall story appears in these pages as I remember it.

# PREFACE

My phone is filled with text messages from dead people. Every so often, I find myself scrolling past daily conversations—with my wife, my daughter, and the various other people in my life—to click on Marci's name. She was the sweet older lady from Michigan who didn't want to show her husband how afraid she was. I knew she was waiting for new results from her doctor whenever I got the text: *Can I vent to you a little bit?*

Or I'll click on Pat's name. He was the Iraq veteran who asked me a question about every detail of his diagnosis. He punctuated each text message about his current bowel movements with a strange *lol.* He was chipper until the end.

Then there was Kevin, the mid-forties divorced guy whose string of five questions in each text conveyed a constant anxiety, bordering on panic. Half of his texts were scary links to various web pages. I imagined he spent more time Googling his survival chances than he actually did trying to survive. None of it ended up mattering.

These people whose text messages fill my phone died because that's what you're supposed to do when you get stomach cancer. This book—written by one of the few people to survive this disease— is dedicated to them. It's also dedicated to the people in my life who did all the little things that helped me survive: Tanya, my many friends new and old, my ex-wife, and above all, my daughter—my light.

# PART ONE

PART ONE

# CHAPTER
# ONE

I stood with my hands on my knees, halfway up the stone staircase that would take us to the top of the Great Wall of China. My chest was tight, my breath stuck. Jen, wearing the yoga pants and sneakers she'd bought just before we set off on this trip, marched five more steps before she realized I wasn't following. She stopped with her hands on her hips and turned around.

"You okay, Steve?" she called from above.

"Yeah," I said. "Just feeling a little sick."

She stood staring at me for several seconds. I could tell her gears were turning with the obvious thoughts: that I'd partied too hard last night with her co-workers. That I should have come to bed at 9 p.m., like she had.

Finally, she responded. "Do you want to go back?"

"No, no. Go ahead. I'll just take some photos down here."

She hesitated, but then her eyes shifted upward to see our tour group charging up the steps ahead. "Well, stay around here so I can find you. My cell phone isn't working up here."

I didn't want to be left alone down there. But how selfish would I seem if I forced her to miss seeing one of the seven wonders of the world because I was hungover? I'd never live it down.

"I'll stay by this thing over here," I said, pointing to a cone-shaped turret jutting out from the side of the wall. She nodded and raced up the steps.

My skin was burning in the late spring sun, and my head ached. I walked to the structure and sat on a shady bench inside, swallowing a few gulps of water to quell the acid feeling in my throat. My stomach churned, and I briefly considered that I might need to find a trash can to throw up in on the Great Wall of China, in front of hundreds of other people. But I swallowed a few times, and the feeling settled.

Through a spy-hole, I could see the expansive wall twisting and turning, seemingly at random, on top of lush green hills that rolled over the horizon. I thought for a second of how crazy it would be to build something like this today. Back home in California, Jen and I were in the middle of our own building project remodeling our house. But the most physical action we took was pointing at pictures of a range stove and a marble countertop.

Still, Jen and I supposedly had *made it*. After years of striving, of positivity and grinding and wishful thinking, we were basically living our dreams. We had the house on the hill in the wealthy enclave of Tiburon, we had our daughter, and we were seeing the world.

But when we got the house, we dreamed of remodeling it. Once we had our first child, Mia, we dreamed of our second. And while we sat in first class on a free flight to China, courtesy of a sales incentive from Jen's company, we talked about how next time we wanted to go on an African safari.

Looking up at the fifty or so stairs above me on the Great Wall, I felt self-conscious, like there was something we just hadn't reached yet, something that was right on the edge of my fingertips that I couldn't figure out.

*Maybe what's missing is that you're sitting down here instead of at the top of the Great Wall of China, you wimp.*

I thought several times of just gritting my teeth and climbing the stairs, just to prove to myself and to anyone else that I could do it, but I knew it would be next to impossible to find Jen in the throngs of thousands of tourists. So, I sat at the turret for thirty minutes, watching old people and children climb to the top of the stairs. I wondered how I, a former varsity athlete in his mid-thirties with no health issues, was still stuck down here just because of a hangover. Was my drinking starting to catch up to me? Could I really keep partying my way through life?

Finally, Jen and the rest of the tour came strolling back down the stairs, their smiling faces telling me they'd just seen a once-in-a-lifetime thing that I'd never know. I melded into the crowd next to Jen, who glanced sideways at me and kept walking.

"How was it up there?" I asked. "Did you feel puny or colossal?"

Finally, she smiled at me. "A little of both. I took some pictures for you up there. How are you feeling?"

"I'm doing better," I said, even as the burning continued to swirl through my abdomen. "I don't know what happened to me."

We walked side by side back toward the bus, Jen listening to the tour guide while I sat in my thoughts. I was afraid that a part of my life was coming to an end, that karma was finally catching up to me. I wondered how I was going to explain to people that the reason I wasn't in any of our pictures was because I couldn't make it to the top of the Great Wall of China.

\* \* \*

We flew back home two days later and went straight to Jen's parents' house to pick up Mia. Before we had left for China, we couldn't wait to have a little bit of time off from the constant needs of a six-month-old child. It felt like a once in a lifetime trip and Mia was only eating and sleeping at this point, so what's the harm in leaving for a few days. But now that we had been gone for a week, all Jen and I could talk about was Mia: whether Jen's parents were feeding her right, whether she could understand enough to miss us, and on and on.

My mother-in-law greeted us at the door with Mia nuzzled up to her chest, asleep.

"Ohh, come here baby," Jen said, reaching out her arms. She held Mia tight into her chest, and I rubbed her smooth forehead. Mia opened her impossible blue eyes and flashed a big, toothless smile before melting into Jen. We strapped her into her car seat and sat in a happy silence as I drove us home. Then Mia pooped in the car, and we had to change her diaper on the side of Highway 101.

I pulled into the driveway of the apartment we were renting while the home was still in a remodel.

We were living temporarily in a one-bedroom apartment, complete with pristine, solid black-and-white furniture that looked straight out of an IKEA box, while our house was under construction. We had only expected to be there a few months, but delays on the project piled up, and at this point it had been almost half a year. The apartment didn't have a baby room, so we kept Mia in a corner of our room. Jen and I both liked to have space to spread out in, and tensions would periodically flare up between us.

Still, that remodel symbolized everything good about our relationship. The house was high up on the hill in a one-percenter town called Tiburon. We bought it using money I received when my adoptive father died. Our expensive renovation included plans for a massive wine cellar that could fit hundreds of bottles. Jen would have a big office upstairs, and the back deck overlooked the bay, with clear views of the rolling hills in the East Bay. It was going to be *perfect.*

Then I got a 9 a.m. phone call.

"Is this Mr. Melen?"

"Yes, who is this?"

"This is Officer Gates with the Tiburon Police Department. Are you the owner of the home on Nathan Way?"

"Yes," I responded. "What's the problem?"

"We need you to come down here as soon as you can. We think there was a break-in."

I hung up the phone. Jen was already awake. "We have to go back to the house," I explained the phone call.

"What the hell? What are we going to do about Mia?"

"Should we bring her with us?" I asked.

"To our house, a crime scene?"

"What else could we do? I think we both need to go, to see what's missing."

We ultimately decided we would have to bring her. We hurriedly strapped her into the car seat, and I sped on the windy two-lane road home.

Jen held Mia as I spoke with the police. Apparently, someone had smashed in one of the windows and stolen the TV by the front door, along with all of Jen's purses and jewelry stashed away deeper in the house. It was the type of crime scene that seemed like someone just *knew* where to look. Suddenly, this dream home didn't feel *quiet* or *out of the way*. It felt *isolated*.

Jen and I stood uncomfortably in the foyer of the home. I wasn't sure how to comfort her, and she seemed the same. We didn't hug. We didn't cry.

"What should we do?" I asked.

"Let's take photos for the insurance company."

As we walked around the house taking photos of every upturned piece of furniture, something felt off between the two of us. Wasn't this the time when you're supposed to feel emotional, to come together as a family? We were a team, but were we a husband and wife?

* * *

Jen and I first met at the tail-end of our 20s, that time of life marked by transition, ambition, and life's big reality checks.

After college, I started working at a financial firm in San Francisco and slowly worked my way up the ranks. I was always the kind of person who needed a *go, go, go* mentality in a workspace, and I found the constant shifting nature and speed of the stock market fit well with me.

I dated a few girls who I liked, but no one who could really check enough boxes for me to feel like I wanted to marry them. On Memorial Day in 1999, I went with some friends down to a hotel in Cabo San Lucas called the Melia. While sitting poolside, I saw a girl who went to my high school in the pool with four other girls, including Jen. We all were introduced and spent the weekend partying and drinking together. I found out Jen lived in the city with some friends, and we exchanged numbers to meet up.

That summer ended up being one of the craziest of my life, as I ran with the bulls in Pamplona and traveled around France, partying at every beach I came to.

Late that summer in Las Vegas, I ran into Jen, who was with her boyfriend. We all got together at a club, and Jen and I spent a long time drinking Long Island iced teas and talking about ourselves. She was a workaholic, just like me. We were both ambitious but family oriented.

Jen's friend came up to me and asked why we weren't dating.

"I mean, I wish. But she has a boyfriend."

Her friend gave me a look as if to say, *don't worry about that.* Sure enough, a few months later the boyfriend was gone, and Jen invited me to Lake Tahoe.

On that trip, we found we both wanted the same things out of life. She wanted two kids, to have a big house and to travel. We had fun almost every second of every day. She was attractive, successful, and upbeat.

We dated for a year when, in 2002, my adoptive father died of a heart attack, just over a decade after my adoptive mother had died of the same thing. Jen was there for me and was a steel girder of support, always offering to take care of this and that and the other thing.

Our relationship was not one based in the past. We never talked about our history. When I started having panic attacks shortly after they died, she never asked me if that was the reason why. She never asked if maybe it was because I was adopted in the first place, that an abandonment like that, even as a baby, might leave an inerasable scar. Instead, it was: "Do you think you need to go on medication? Are you telling your therapist everything that's going on?"

Likewise, I never felt comfortable asking Jen about her past. I knew she didn't have many friends from college or before that, because when we took trips, it was always with my friends. Our relationship was all covered in a blanket of positivity, of striving for the future.

Nonetheless, as I moved into my 30's with both of my parents gone, I felt like the patriarch of my family and I decided it was time to settle down. We got married in 2003 and waited a year before trying to have kids. Those times were filled with hope and success as we both climbed our respective career ladders. Almost every afternoon, we would take a walk around our neighborhood, talking about friends, family and what we wanted out of life. Even when our conversations were frustrated, focusing on the trial of the individual day, we had an invincible spirit. We felt unstoppable, like life could only go *up, up, up.*

# CHAPTER
# TWO

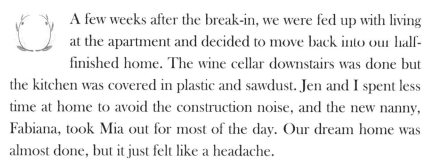 A few weeks after the break-in, we were fed up with living at the apartment and decided to move back into our half-finished home. The wine cellar downstairs was done but the kitchen was covered in plastic and sawdust. Jen and I spent less time at home to avoid the construction noise, and the new nanny, Fabiana, took Mia out for most of the day. Our dream home was almost done, but it just felt like a headache.

A couple weeks after we returned back from China, I got a new job as a financial advisor for MS Wealth Management, moving over from another firm in San Francisco. The new job gave me a lot more flexibility, but I could feel the pressure to perform as the new guy. I worked more than sixty hours in my first weeks, starting my days at 5 a.m. when the stock market opened and ending well after 5 p.m.

On one Thursday morning, I was sitting at my desk, my jaw clenched from chugging two cups of coffee and sending out ten emails in a row, when my chest tightened. My stomach suddenly felt like it was a volcano shooting lava up into my throat. It was almost the exact same feeling from the Great Wall, and this time I hadn't been drinking the night before. *Weird.* I burped a few times and then almost puked, but I swallowed to hold it back. I drank a glass of water, and the pain quieted into a discomfort. When I tried to eat my lunch, the bites stuck in the bottom of my throat like a car stuck in a traffic jam. Something was clogging up the roadway.

I went to my manager's office.

"Hey, I think I ate something bad for lunch. Okay if I head home a bit early?"

"Yeah, no problem," she said. "You've been doing great since joining the team. Go get some rest."

I smiled and gathered together my stuff. When I got home, Jen was pumping milk on the couch.

"Are you heading out of town this weekend?" I asked.

"Yes, I already told you. They're sending me up to Seattle for a client meeting."

"Oh, okay." I was secretly glad I'd have the house to myself for a few days. "Is Mia in her crib?"

"She's sleeping. Fabiana says she's been missing her naps during the day lately."

"Mm. I knew she wasn't going to sleep twenty-two hours a day forever."

I turned on the TV and flipped over to the news. Jen checked her emails with one hand and pumped milk with the other.

"Why are you home early?" she asked.

"I had that acid reflux thing flare up again."

"When was the last time that happened?"

"A couple of days ago."

"You're probably just stressed."

"I don't know. Yeah. I guess maybe it is stress. I'll probably be fine."

We sat for an hour in front of the TV, absorbed in our own inner lives, a chasm the space of a couch cushion in between us. Was this what being a parent was like? Not really communicating, just having bite-sized conversations in front of the TV until we had something else to do for Mia?

As the pain continued through the night, I thought of all the times I woke up with a sour stomach after a night of drinking. I went down into the cellar, which buzzed with the sound of the 24-hour generator that kept it chilled at exactly 55 degrees. I picked a bottle of Cabernet from the half-full shelf, then poured a glass in the kitchen.

I drank half the glass in one gulp. A burp, and then the burning feeling in my stomach went away. *Why does alcohol always make things better?*

\* \* \*

Over the next few weeks, those evening glasses of wine were the only thing I could look forward to. When I woke up every morning at 4:30 a.m., I could already feel that lump lodged in my stomach. Coffee helped soothe it temporarily, softening up my throat like moistening a piece of leather. Instead of my usual big breakfasts of bacon and eggs, I'd get a muffin at one of the stores downtown before heading into work.

Then, I would meet with clients all day until I came home around 4 or 5 p.m. By that point, the feeling had flared up again, so I would switch from coffee to wine, heading down to my new cellar to uncork another bottle. Two glasses would do the trick, and then I would feel okay enough to eat dinner. Finally, I'd go into the baby room and lean over Mia's crib. Usually, she just kept sleeping, her mouth open and her legs twisting in a dream. But occasionally, she'd wake up and would stare directly into my eyes. I felt so happy in those moments, like I had finally figured out what was going to fulfill me. But I also felt worried. Was I taking care of myself well enough? Was I doing my part to keep myself healthy so I could take care of her? When I looked into her eyes, I knew, somehow, that I wasn't.

After that feeling percolated for a few weeks, I finally went to see my primary care physician, Dr. Hahn, over at California Pacific

Medical Center. I had been seeing him for 20 years, so he knew everything about me.

"What's been going on, Steve? How's your daughter?"

"She's great. It's an endless cycle of poop, eat, sleep for her. I'm kind of jealous."

"It's the life, isn't it? What's going on today?"

"I've been feeling this pain in my chest for the past two or so months. It feels like acid reflux, but it's just *constant* now. I don't know if it's stress-related, or if my roaring 20's are starting to catch up with me."

"Hm, okay. And what else has been going on for you?"

"Oh, man. You want the laundry list?"

"I wouldn't expect anything less from you, Steve."

I told him about the remodel, the break-in, the new baby, the new job. I didn't even realize just how much was going on, how stressed I was, until I said it all aloud.

"So, I think you're right, that this is more about stress than anything," he said. "It'll definitely be something we want to keep monitoring, but I think you just need to take some stuff off your plate. I'm going to prescribe you some Protonix for acid reflux in the meantime."

"Thanks a ton, Dr. Hahn," I said. "I really needed this."

After that visit, I had an excuse every time I felt the pain in my stomach. *Oh, it's just because I had a shitty call with a client. It's just because this or that.* Whatever.

But over the next few months, things got progressively worse. The pain started to keep me awake at night, forcing me to sleep on my back instead of my stomach. When the morning came, coffee barely did anything to help. I was completely out of energy by lunchtime. I told myself that I needed to keep lowering my stress and started leaving work at 3 p.m. instead of 5 p.m. Then I started to leave at 2 p.m. instead of 3 p.m., and I would go to Poppi's Pizza on Lombard Street to have a glass of wine before heading home. I'd tell my boss I was in client meetings all day, when actually I was sitting alone at the bar, trying to soothe the pain.

One night in October while lying in bed, Jen grabbed me around the arm and seemed surprised by what she felt.

"Have you weighed yourself recently?"

"No, I haven't. But I know I've lost weight. It's been hard to get food down."

"I'm starting to get worried about you. You don't seem like you have as much energy lately."

"I'm just trying to keep my stress down, like the doctor said."

"I don't know. Something else just feels different."

"Yeah." Hearing that what was going on with me was noticeable to other people scared me. Who else had seen me change? My boss? "To be honest, I'm a little scared."

"Oh, Steve, it's going to be okay. I'm not trying to scare you. I just think you need to go check back in with your doctor. You might have an ulcer."

"Yeah. Maybe that's it."

A few days later, Dr. Hahn took some bloodwork to test for an ulcer. It came back negative, and he told me, once again, to lower my stress. I left with another prescription for Protonix, and a prescription to tell myself that everything was fine, and this would all pass eventually.

I continued to go through the motions of my life, spending day after day looking three feet in front of me at whatever my next task was. I was afraid to look up, to take stock of everything and admit to myself that something was really wrong.

Then, in December, I got a text message from Chris, one of my college friends. He was our fraternity president, one of those guys who just seemed to coast through life, winning at everything.

"Melen. Palm Springs in two weeks. All of the guys are gonna get back together. You in?"

*God I need this,* I thought. Everything up until that point had been so serious—the pain, the wife, the baby, the job. I didn't feel like myself. I was usually fun, the person who brought the party, who kept it going. I wasn't the person who sulked at home alone at night.

I responded immediately: "Hell yeah. I'm in."

I booked my trip to Palm Springs and then asked Jen. She pursed her lips and said: "Have fun."

I hopped on my flight with the giddiness of a teenager who gets left home alone for the first time. I felt like I could still escape if I needed to. Even if I wasn't necessarily *going* to escape, I still could. I ignored the pain still throbbing in my chest.

Even though it was December, waves of heat radiated off the asphalt as I took a taxi from the airport to Chris' house, which was a villa on a golf course in La Quinta.

He greeted me with a fist bump and a margarita.

"Melen! What's up, man? How you been?"

"Never better. I haven't seen this place before. It's amazing!"

We walked to the pool, where three of the guys were already sitting. The sparkling blue of the water was a stunning contrast against the desert landscape. We all got on pool floaties with cocktails in hand and reminisced on college — who had gotten married to whom, our favorite parties, the worst classes we took. Everything that had been on my shoulders was relaxed, and for the first time in months I felt weightless.

About an hour and two drinks after I got there, the doorbell rang. We went out front and greeted Rick, who was a hairless, comically muscular Italian and the alpha of our group. He walked in yelling greetings and aggressively smacking everyone's back.

"Holy shit, what's the matter with you?" Rick said to me. "You look pale, dude. Like, *yellow.*"

Suddenly I felt anxious. *Is it really that noticeable?* I forced a laugh. "Hangovers do that to me."

His legs moved like they were on a trolley track, heading to the bar for his first drink of the trip. "Well, then, you better get a drink in your hand. Get some color on that buttery face."

He went straight for the Jose Cuervo and skipped the margarita glasses, pouring out seven shots instead.

"Woah now, getting going early, huh?" I said.

"You kidding? This is the only vacation I'm gonna get in six months. Drink Up, chicken arms!"

We each took a shot glass and stood around in a circle. I shivered at what was about to happen to me. *Am I going to throw up? These guys will never let me live it down.* We clinked our glasses together and all shouted something indecipherable even to ourselves, and then I tipped the shot up. I thought of just holding the liquid in my mouth and spitting it in the sink, but I knew this wasn't the time for half measures. I swallowed the shot and immediately bent over, coughing five times and making a sound like I had just eaten a ghost pepper. *Eeeyuck.* I turned around to head for the sink, but the need to vomit passed, and I rejoined the group.

"Meeeelen, can't hang anymore?" Chris said.

"Been a while for tequila shots. Having a kid's got me feeling old."

"Hey, how old is she now?"

"Just over one year. Little goddamn ball of sunshine. I love her so much."

A few minutes later, Chris pulled me aside.

"You know I was just messing with you. But, man, you really do look a little sick. You been okay?"

"Yeah, I'm fine," I said, wishing that this would stop. This trip was supposed to be my escape. I didn't want to answer any more questions. "It's just been a stressful time lately, and I haven't been getting enough sleep. I'm fine. I'm fine."

Chris looked at me for several seconds. "Alright, well we're here for you man. For real."

"Thanks, I appreciate it. Right now, I just don't want to think about any of the stressful shit."

And after that, I didn't think about it. This trip felt like my chance to grasp at the last bit of my youth and deal with the consequences of whatever was going on with me later. Every night, we hit the strip of bars downtown. The warmth of each shot did a little more work to numb the pain away until I just lost myself to being with my best friends. It would just come back with a vengeance in the morning, but a tequila sunrise always did the trick. We did this for three days straight, until it was time to head back to our lives.

When I hugged Chris goodbye, he had a worried look on his face again.

"You know, Steve, I don't want to keep bringing this up, but you really do look a little yellow."

# CHAPTER
# THREE

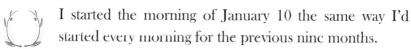 I started the morning of January 10 the same way I'd started every morning for the previous nine months.

I climbed into my custom-fit dress shirt that now hung over my body like a loose night-shirt. I cinched my belt to the last notch. After a coffee, I drove to the office, where Karen, the young woman who worked at the front desk, greeted me as Mr. Melen.

I walked past a half-dozen work desks to get to my office. It was strange; I was usually one of the most outgoing people in an office, but after half a year working here, I still felt like I didn't really know these people.

At 11 a.m., the HR head knocked on the door and walked into my office.

"Korean barbecue for lunch today. Come by the conference room at noon."

"Korean barbecue? That's different."

I sat at my computer for the next hour in a haze, as the numbers of stock market reports switched around on my screen. This had been happening in the past few weeks. I'd start to get extremely tired halfway through the day and just couldn't focus on the most basic parts of my job.

At noon, I went to the communal table and quickly grabbed my plate of food before heading back to eat at my desk and finish the day's work.

I wasn't even really sure what was on my plate, but I grabbed a forkful of some saucy meat and took a bite. It seemed to grind down my throat and hit something in my body like a lump. I exhaled. *That didn't feel right.* Sweat started to form on my face as I tried to take another bite. Same feeling.

I got an intense sensation that I needed to vomit. *Now.* I jumped out of my chair, grabbed the trash can, and in a second threw up the bite I had taken. In the trash can, the barely digested food sat shamefully on top of an open piece of mail.

Something felt really, horribly wrong. Most 37-year-old men didn't just vomit at work from eating Korean food. *What the hell is the matter with me?*

I wiped my mouth and looked over to my office door. Thankfully, it was closed. No one saw what just happened. I made a beeline for the front door, without looking at any co-workers and went straight home.

Jen was out of town again. Fabiana was in the kitchen cutting carrots for Mia, who bounced up and down in her highchair. Mia smiled and giggled when she saw me.

"Hi, Mr. Melen," Fabiana said, flashing a wide, toothy smile. Fabiana was our best nanny yet. She had just come to the U.S. from Brazil, and she was always on time and cared for Mia like she was her own.

"Hi Fabiana. How are you?"

"Estoy bien," she said, facing Mia. Jen and I wanted Mia to learn Spanish, so we asked Fabiana to speak it as much as she could. But since neither of us spoke the language fluently, we never knew if she was speaking Spanish or Portuguese or half and half.

"I took Mia to the park this morning, she said, then looked at me. "Are you feeling okay? You look a little tired."

"I'm a little nauseous from lunch today. I'm going to stay home, so you can take the rest of the day off."

She picked up Mia and kissed her on the nose.

"Buenas tardes, mi amor."

I watched her leave, then grimaced and hunched over the table in pain. Mia bounced in her chair. I tried to gather myself and puffed out my cheeks at her. She giggled.

An open bottle of cabernet sat on the counter. I poured a quarter of the bottle into a souvenir Giants cup and took a gulp, hoping it would quell my stomach so I could eat.

Food sounded horrible, but I thought I might need to eat, so I flopped a tortilla onto a pan and spread some cheese on top. Then I took a bite, but the food hit that same spot in my throat. I tried to gulp down one more bite, but it felt worse. I gagged.

The sound of Mia winding up for a good cry shook me out of my head. *You've got someone else to take care of.*

I picked Mia up and held her in my forearms. Her wails got louder and louder.

"You hungry, baby girl?"

I got Jen's milk out of the fridge and held the bottle at her mouth. I already felt nauseous and now, for the first time, I felt like I could *smell* the milk. And then I remembered that I was feeding my child *milk* that came out of *my wife* and that having a kid is *fucking weird,* and I thought I was about to puke right on top of my baby's head. I made a *hlluurp* sound that seemed to come from some alien creature in the bottom of my throat. I put Mia on my knees and fed her with one hand, plugging my nose with the other.

I only gave her half the amount I normally would and put her in her crib. She squirmed with energy.

"Please, just go to sleep," I begged the uncomprehending baby below me.

I brought her baby monitor out to the deck and sat there drinking my cup of wine, scared into near paralysis.

"I'll be okay, I'll be okay," I said out loud, repeating the words my therapist had told me might help back when I got panic attacks in my 20s.

*Maybe tomorrow will be a new day,* I thought. *Maybe I'll feel better. It could have just been that Korean barbecue.*

I finished my wine and went to watch TV in bed, placing Mia's monitor on my nightstand.

After I spent a whole night tossing around in bed feeling a constant, low-level pain that became all-encompassing in its mundane throbbing, the sun rose, and I still felt terrible and now exhausted, too. *Nothing had changed.*

I knew I had to eat something, or get some sleep, or do *something* different. Jen was flying back home and didn't have her phone on. I texted Fabiana to see if she could pick me up some Pepto-Bismol on her way to the house. When she arrived around 8 a.m., I drank more than a quarter of it straight from the bottle. It still didn't help. I had no idea what to do. I felt completely alone.

Finally, I drove myself to the ER at Marin General Hospital.

The doctor, a tall Asian woman, hooked me up to an IV, telling me they were concerned about dehydration. Then she did some tests, and I lay in a fog until she came back in with a worried look on her face.

"The tests came back, and they show that you're anemic," she said. "Pretty severely. Have you had surgery recently?"

*Anemic? What does that even mean? What's wrong with me?*

"No," I replied.

"Have you had any blood in your stool?"

"Not that I've noticed. What do you think is going on?"

She flipped the chart and looked at me. "Well, it's almost like you're bleeding internally."

I could feel my heart beating double-time. "Uh, that sounds bad."

"We aren't sure yet. We're going to need to do some more tests, starting with a chest scan."

They wheeled me, still in my hospital bed, into a room with a giant machine that looked suitable for space travel. A nurse pushed me inside. I looked at the curved white cylinder above me, numb, feeling completely out of control of my life.

The machine sprang to life with a *zaaaaaaaap* followed by a satisfied *beep!* Within a few seconds the nurse took me out of the white tunnel and wheeled me back down the hall.

I sat alone on the stiff bed staring at the blank walls, trying to remember what my Biology 101 professor in college said about the word *anemia.* Then I remembered Jen was due to arrive at San Francisco International in two hours. I started to pull out my phone, but the doctor came into the room again, that same concerned look on her face.

"We see something in there, and it doesn't look right," she said to me.

"Okay? How not right?"

"It's hard to say for now. We are going to have you do an endoscopy."

"When are we going to have any answers? I've been here for hours."

"Right now, we're working on ruling things out. This is all part of the process."

I felt impatient and scared. I didn't have anyone to talk to, no one to give me advice or calm my nerves.

"Endoscopy?" I said. "Is that the one where you stick a camera up my butt? ... Er, through my rectum?"

She didn't smile. "Other end. We'll put a tiny tube with a camera down your throat."

"Oh, god. Is that painful? When do I have to have that done?"

"We will sedate you before we start. And right now."

I wasn't prepared for this. Just few hours ago, I was at home in my bed, and now I had to be sedated and have a camera shoved down my throat? *No one even knows I'm here right now, except the nanny.*

Before I could say anything, another nurse came into the room and unlocked the wheels on my bed, then rolled me through an elevator and up to a big, empty room.

My vision blurred as the white walls started to feel blinding. A man's face with a respirator appeared right in front of my face. His disembodied voice told me to count down from ten as he injected the anesthesia.

"Ten...." *Is this even happening right now? How am I here?*

"Nine...." *What am I going to feel like when I wake up from this?*

"Eight ..." *How is anyone going to know to pick me up from the hospital?*

"Sev—"

*Out.*

\* \* \*

I woke up to the sound of a high-pitched whine from somewhere distant. My throat felt like it had been rubbed with sandpaper. A door opened, and in walked my doctor, flipping through a chart. She lowered it and walked toward me, her heels clonking on the floor.

"Can you tell me your name?"

"Steve — Steven Melen."

"And what year is it, Steve?"

"January ... or, uh, 2008."

"I've got some bad news." She sighed. "It looks like you may have cancer."

Everything slowed down as I leaned my head back onto the pillow behind me. I closed my eyes and feelings of complete numbness, a total lack of thought, an inability to speak, overtook me. My whole life seemed to be spread in front of me like a deck of cards: where I came from, who I had become, how much I still hadn't done ...

*Oh. Shit.*

"What? What do you mean? What kind of cancer?"

"You've got a five-centimeter mass near your gastroesophageal junction. At the base of your esophagus. And it's bleeding, so that's why you're anemic. We need to take care of this right away."

She kept talking, but I barely listened. Weirdly, I didn't think about dying. I didn't even cry. I was just angry. *Why the hell is this happening? I could've gotten cancer when I was 70, and then sure, whatever, fine. But I've got too much shit going on right now. I don't need this.*

I nodded a few rote affirmations of whatever the doctor said, and she left the room. I checked the time: 3:30 p.m. Jen would be landing in 30 minutes. I pulled out my phone to text her. I wasn't sure whether to tell her everything now or wait. If I told her something was wrong but was too vague, it'd leave her mind to wander to the worst-case scenario. But if I just told her I had cancer, she might have a panic attack on the tarmac. And who delivers this kind of news in a text message?

"Been at the hospital for the past few hours," I wrote. "I got some bad news from the doctor. Heading home. Talk soon. I love you."

I felt strange delivering some of the most consequential information of my life to a cell phone that was turned off. It was anticlimactic. Halfway home from the hospital, I got a text back from Jen.

"Omg. I'm so sorry. I'll be home in a few."

We got back at almost the same time, and when I opened the front door, Jen rushed into the foyer and hugged me. We held it for a long time. As she clutched at my shirt around my back, I tried to remember the last time we had hugged for this long.

She let go and looked at me. "Steve, what is it?"

"I — I think I have cancer."

She gasped. "Oh my god. Oh my god."

"But they don't know how bad it is. All I know is I have to go see a specialist to figure out what to do."

She put her hands over her eyes and started sobbing, long wails that were deeper than anything I had ever heard from her. She breathed in and tried to gather herself.

"We can deal with this," she said, her voice quivering. "We can get through this."

"Yeah, we can." It almost made me feel better, but when I looked at her face, I could tell that ever-stoic Jen was completely panicked.

\* \* \*

The next two days were a blur of phone calls. Jen went into overdrive, calling every single contact she had, trying to find out what the hell we should do based on what we knew. I could hear her anxiety every time she repeated: "It's cancer, somewhere in his esophagus. No, we're not sure what stage yet." During the day, we both tried to stay strong so Mia wouldn't see us crying. At night, we hugged in bed and let it out.

Soon, Jen had booked me three appointments at three different hospitals to figure out exactly how much shit I was in.

At my first appointment at California Pacific Medical Center, after they sedated me again to stick another camera down my throat, the oncologist told me my diagnosis.

"You have Stage IIIB stomach cancer."

He said it with a severity that made me think this was supposed to be bad news, but I was actually relieved. The only thing I knew at the time about cancer was that Stage IV was really, really bad. So at least I was one number removed from that.

"What we should do," he said, "is take out your stomach. The cancerous cells have spread too far in there. Then we'll need to do chemotherapy and radiation to make sure we've gotten it everywhere else it might have spread."

"Hold on a second ... Take out my stomach? You want to take out my stomach?"

"Yes. It might seem shocking, but it's a surgery that's becoming more and more common. Many people are actually able to live relatively normal lives without a stomach."

"Um. I think I need some time to process this."

I left that appointment skeptical, in disbelief that I would actually be able to live any sort of "normal" life without a stomach. I'd probably end up being one of those guys whose wife has to change his diaper every four hours. *I'll pass,* I thought, holding out hope that my next appointments would go differently.

Next up was a visit with the head doctor at UCSF, Dr. S.

He elaborated that I had stomach cancer where my stomach connected with my esophagus. He said they wanted to first go and shrink the mass with chemotherapy and radiation. Once it had shrunk, they would decide if they needed to remove part of my stomach.

This was already sounding better to me, but it also scared me that two doctors told me two different approaches. How was I supposed to know who was right? At this point, I just wanted someone to tell me what to do.

Luckily, through a connection Jen had, I got my last appointment scheduled with Dr. N, the chief of the oncology department at Stanford University. Not just Stanford, to me, but *The. Cardinal.* Stanford was the shining beacon of my youth, the place where my dad and uncle both got their higher degrees. The place I couldn't get into because I goofed off too much in high school. Stanford was synonymous, in my mind, with success. Dr. N seemed to epitomize that, as he was renowned for successful stomach surgeries on late-stage cancer patients.

I thought to myself, wouldn't it be funny if this was the way I got admitted into Stanford—on a hospital bed.

I got in to see Dr. N for a consultation via a sort of VIP group called Special Patient Services, which is like this secret exclusive club of well-connected cancer patients. I got free valet parking and bagels in the waiting room. I felt like I should have been wearing a suit and tie, instead of my hoodie and jeans.

The nurse greeted me like I was a celebrity and ran some tests. Then I went in to a large, wood-paneled office to see Dr. N and Dr. F, who was an oncologist with the department. It felt like I was there to give them financial advice, not get a cancer diagnosis.

"We think the best course is to be aggressive," said Dr. N. "Your pancreas is swollen, meaning it is possible the cancer may have spread there. We are going to take out your stomach and half of your pancreas. Then we'll do a strong routine of chemotherapy and radiation."

"And how dangerous is the surgery?" I asked, almost hoping they wouldn't answer.

"I won't sugar-coat it. There's probably about a five percent chance you won't make it through the surgery."

"Oh."

"I know that isn't easy to hear. And this is not going to be easy, but it will be the best way to make sure that it doesn't come back, and that you can live a healthy life in the future."

I left that meeting unable to get the words *five percent* out of my head. This wasn't a roulette wheel, with death on Fourteen Black. This was a game of craps. Roll a three, and I'm dead.

Throughout my life, I had tried to be in firm control of everything happening to me. I did X because of Y, I failed at *this* because I didn't do *that*. I succeeded at the other thing because of the work I put in.

But now, I had cancer because of ... ? What had I done to deserve this? And now I had to make a decision between three different doctors, all of whom very confidently gave me their opinions of what I should do based on some knowledge that I would never understand. How is anyone supposed to decide on this?

Later that evening, I sat in the living room and closed my eyes. The only thing I could do was make a choice and embrace it as the only choice I ever could have made. I said my choice, out loud, to no one. "Alright, The Cardinal. Here we go."

Once I said that, it all finally felt real. There would be no waking up and finding out this was all a dream. If I survived at all, my life was about to be completely different. I was going to be living *without a stomach*. I couldn't even really fathom all of the specifics of what that would entail, and the thought made me feel like I had to vomit.

Trying to calm myself down, I went to our bedroom and walked past the king mattress to my nightstand. I pulled out an old, worn U-Haul box marked STEVE MEMORIES. Under photos and trophies, I found what I was looking for: the red firetruck from 1971. Its colors had faded, but the wheels still spun with a click. I thought back to my childhood and remembered what it was like to feel safe, to feel wrapped up in the warmth of a loving family.

The veneer of my life was about to be ripped off, and I was about to see what was really underneath. As I looked at the truck, I felt ready for the challenge. Bring it on.

# CHAPTER

# FOUR

## 1970

I was conceived around senior prom in a tiny rural Minnesota town called Esko. My father, Ron Miilamenen, was an alcoholic in the making, and my mother, Penny Lingo, was a young woman caught in the wrong town at the wrong time.

Penny was marked with a scarlet letter when her out-of-wedlock pregnancy became the talk of town. She had to move to an unwed mothers' home in Minneapolis for her pregnancy. A few months after I was born, she left with me to come live with her dad's side of the family on the east side of San Jose. Before she left, though, she told my biological father that she had gotten in a car accident and I died in the crash. Whether or not he believed her, he never saw fit to check out her claims for himself.

Penny quickly realized that, as an eighteen-year-old high school dropout, she didn't really have any skills and raising a kid was hard without any money. Her family wasn't in financial shape and couldn't help, either. When I was just under a year old, she made the decision to give me up for adoption.

Meanwhile, Bill and Connie Melen, a Silicon Valley couple, had been waiting for years on adoption waitlists before the name Steven

Ray Lingo came to their attention. Connie was a 3rd grade schoolteacher in San Jose where my mom's sister went to school. Connie had told her class that she would love to adopt a child and my biological 3rd grade aunt spoke up and told Mrs. Melen that her half-sister had a little boy she could adopt.

Within days, I was dropped off at the school and my new temporary parents made the exchange of this tiny human being. No paperwork, just a test run, and suddenly I was a new person, Steven Patrick Melen. They buckled me in the back seat of their station wagon and drove straight to Toys-R-Us.

In true Bay Area fashion, they had gone to see a psychologist before bringing me home. The psychologist told them they needed to give me stability, to avoid any further trauma at all costs. With Bill working as an electrical engineer and Connie as a teacher, they thought they could give me that environment. But still, my future parents decided I'd need a token, something I could look at and in my one-year-old mind say, *I have a home now.*

My new father held me while I apparently stared with wide eyes at the fluorescent lights and the massive shelves at the store. This new, unfamiliar man pointed one by one at the items on the shelves, asking if I wanted them.

My face must've told him, *No, not that one, or that one, or that one,* until he finally got to a shiny red fire truck that was almost as big as I was. Something in my young mind must have known *that* was the one and communicated it to him. He grabbed it off the shelf and gave it to me, and I held it all the way home.

Though I don't remember that moment, over the years, looking at that fire truck helped me feel like I was safe, that everything was going to be okay and I was in a stable, loving place. I like to think that feeling came from the scared one-year-old in a big store being held by a stranger who did something nice for him, then gave him a home and stuck around.

My parents did everything they could to make my environment as stable as possible. I grew up in a suburban neighborhood in the city of Saratoga, formed out of a triangle of three major thoroughfares through Silicon Valley. We called it the Golden Triangle. Our street was wide and empty enough to play sports on, and mountains surrounded everything. It felt like my world was framed by those mountains, by those thoroughfares, like I was safe within this little cocoon that had been built for me.

My friends and I lived idyllic childhoods, biking to cherry orchards and jumping over dirt ramps, then heading to the corner store for ice cream. My parents left the keys in the station wagon at night, and even after someone stole the station wagon, they shrugged and kept their trusting spirit. We lived quintessential American lives in a quintessential American neighborhood.

In following everything the psychologist recommended when it came to an adopted child, though, my parents spoiled me. I had the nicest bike on the block and brought turkey sandwiches for lunch every day while everyone else had PB&Js. I was quick with my wits, and over time I'd learn how to game their willingness to give me whatever I wanted.

The cliché story for adopted kids is that one day when you're eight or so years old, your parents sit you down for a talk and break the news: "Billy, you're different from the rest of the kids. You were adopted."

This never happened for me. From the moment I set foot in the Melen home, I was told that I was special, that I was extra loved, precisely *because* I was adopted.

I really tried to embrace it as I moved into elementary school.

"I'm adopted. That means my parents had to actually pick me," I'd tell any classmates that tried to poke fun at me. "You were just an accident."

That's how I was. I was talkative, I was funny, and I could deflect. But there was something deep inside of me that said I was unwanted, that someone gave me away and that someone would always want to give me away. It's hard to be an adopted kid and not feel that on a certain level. My jokey attitude was all coping, trying to get ahead of the stories people might tell about me.

The feeling percolated under the surface as I grew into a skinny, tall, athletic kid. But I could keep it there, in the unspoken realm, as I pursued the various chases of growing up: friends, sports, girls, alcohol. I was popular and became a varsity athlete, and I lost my virginity to an older girl from my school named Tanya, when I was a senior.

But with time, things bubbled up. For one, something always looked out of place when my parents and I were together: they were both obese and round-faced, while I was a tall, skinny Scandinavian kid with pronounced angular features. I always felt just so physically and obviously different from them that I could never entirely be theirs.

And as a teenager, I started to resent how rosy my parents kept everything. The conversation *always* had to stay positive. My mom had a habit of shaking her head and quickly—too quickly—changing the subject whenever something negative came up. It may have been well-intentioned, but it all fed my paranoia that my life was a carefully constructed movie set with just planks of wood holding up the pretty exteriors. The lengths that everyone went to protect me just made me feel hollow. I intentionally brought up negative things in order to push her buttons.

I felt a pull, a desire to deconstruct this movie set of my life. I toyed with the idea of meeting my biological mom. I wondered what she would look like, her tics, if she ate the same food as me. But at the same time, I didn't want to take the leap and hurt my parents. I could tell they were afraid that after they gave me everything, I would one day choose to leave and rejoin my biological mom.

So, I went through seventeen years of my life in a constant state of low-level curiosity. I wondered what there was to find out about this woman but was afraid, for myself and for my parents, to actually pick up the phone.

It all changed in my senior year of high school, in February of 1988. I had just turned eighteen, and I was late for school because I had accidentally packed the wrong surfboard into my red pickup truck.

I peeled into the school's parking lot and jerked into a spot as close as possible to the building. I looked at the clock—still five minutes until first period, ceramics, which was a blow-off class anyway. I took a deep breath and gathered myself, looking to walk inside with the feigned nonchalance all high schoolers strive for.

I opened my car door and started to get out, but as I turned my head, I saw a woman a couple parking spots away. She was walking toward me—walking directly toward me. She definitely wasn't in high school. She looked like she was in her mid-thirties, with blonde hair and a tall face with a prominent forehead and—*Ohhhhhh, my god. It's her. It's goddamn her. It's fucking herherherher.*

There was no way around it. She looked just like me. She kept walking toward me. I felt like I was going to vomit, and the absurd thought crossed my mind that I was going to have to get a tardy notice from the school administrators. *Late for pottery, met my biological mom for the first time ever,* it would maybe say.

She was right in front of me. The real person. She was younger than my parents, but with weary lines on her face that my parents didn't have.

"Hello, Steven." She said it with so much familiarity, like she was picking me up from summer camp. Then she sniffled, barely holding back tears. "I'm Penny."

I couldn't say words. I couldn't think. What even was there to say—How are you?

We both burst into tears, and we grabbed each other and held as if the other one might disappear if we let go. As if it was all a dream unless we were hugging, and this was what made it real.

"I'm so sorry," she said once she was able to say anything at all.

She started talking excitedly. She probably had a whole speech rehearsed, and now she was spitting it out in a span of five seconds.

"I'm sorry. Your parents never wanted me to reach out to you. But I knew you just turned eighteen, so I wanted to give you the chance to communicate with me if you want to."

She paused, as if waiting for me to say something, but I was dumbfounded.

"I—I—"

Suddenly I thought of my parents and felt guilty. Why should I feel guilty? I didn't arrange any of this. But I thought of the pain, the disappointment they would feel if they knew what was happening in this parking lot.

"You don't ever have to talk to me again," she said, nodding frantically and batting away tears. "But it's all up to you. I just wanted to give you the opportunity. If you ever wanted to know what happened, why I had to—"

She stopped.

I stared at her as she wiped her face. I felt trapped, trapped into this meeting I always wanted but never could have. She was *here*, right here in front of me, and there were so many things I wanted to ask her. But I couldn't even say anything, and I also wanted to go escape and just shape some damn clay or something.

The school bell rang, to my relief. The chime of this little sheltered fantasy world of the school, away from any reality out in this parking lot. Penny jerked toward the source of the sound, too.

"I—I've got to go to class."

She nodded a thousand times. "Mmhmm. Okay." She put her hand to her face, then dropped it. "Here." She handed me a Post-it note with her phone number already written on it. She had been planning for this. "I'll be at Vasona Park this afternoon. Do you know where that is?"

I nodded. It was right on the way to our surf spot in Santa Cruz.

"If you want to meet me there, I'll be waiting."

"Okay. Maybe I'll go. I'm not sure."

"Alright, that's okay. Go ahead to class. I love you, Steven."

I stood unable to say anything other than, "Bye." I scurried away.

I don't remember walking into ceramics class, but I must've been late. A guy in my class named Aaron, one of those troublemakers who would always steal things and then laugh at you for getting mad about it, walked over to me. He had apparently seen me in the parking lot.

"Was that one of your girlfriend's moms? Did you get someone pregnant?" Then he laughed at his own joke.

"That was my biological mom." I was in shock, reduced to a dull monotone.

Something jolted in him. "No way. Wait, holy shit—really?"

He was the first person I had told. Something about telling this random clown in my ceramics class before anyone else about the biggest moment of my life almost had me crack up laughing. Instead, I nodded solemnly.

"Oh, shit, man. That's heavy." He turned around and walked back to his seat.

I was in a stupor for the rest of the day. Everything in my life suddenly felt like petty niceties that could just collapse with the softest blow of wind. The house was built without a foundation.

At the end of the day, my friend Dave was waiting for me by his 1963 Mustang to head down to Santa Cruz. I told him what had happened.

"You gotta go meet her, man. You're going to regret it if you don't."

I knew he was right, but it all seemed like it just had so much weight to it. All I wanted to do was surf and chase girls and go off to college. I didn't want to deal with this now.

I took a deep breath.

"Okay, do you mind waiting while I talk to her?"

He agreed, and we put our boards on his surf racks and drove south toward Santa Cruz.

Once we parked, I got out and went over to a trailhead. Penny was sitting there, on a bench right near the entrance to the park. She was jiggling her foot, crossed over her other leg, and picking at her fingernails. She saw me and seemed to take a big breath. We hugged again and lingered.

She spoke first. "I can't believe I'm seeing you here, in person. The only way I've seen you all grown up is in these." She pulled a newspaper out of her purse. It was a copy of the *Saratoga News* from last year with a picture of me on the pitching mound after we won a divisional game.

"It's different when you're not in black-and-white," she said.

"Why would you give me up?" I asked, maybe a little too suddenly, too aggressively. I regretted asking it when I saw the hurt in her eyes.

She had to take a deep, shaky breath before speaking. "I know you'll probably never believe me, but everything I did was for you. I wasn't in a good mental state when I had you. I didn't think I'd be able to give you the home you deserved. But it tore me up to do that, to give you up to some strangers."

"They're my parents now."

"I know, I know. And I'm so appreciative that they've raised you in a happy, loving home. One that I couldn't have given you before." She lowered her head and looked at her mangled fingernails.

"But why reach out now, after all this time?"

"It hurt me so much, having you live just thirty miles away and never seeing you. But I wanted to respect that you were Bill's and Connie's. Anyway, now that you're an adult, I wanted to make it your choice. I don't want it to be anyone else's choice."

If this was what being an adult meant, I wasn't sure I wanted to buy in. I didn't want to make this damn choice! Someone else make the choices for me!

"I—I don't know what to do," I said. "They raised me. I don't want to hurt them."

She put her hand on my leg.

"I understand, Steven. Really, I do. If you never want to hear from me again, you don't have to. I'll just give you my information if you want to reach out again."

She also offered that if I wanted to know anything else about my biological father, she could tell me about him. She could send me pictures.

I didn't think I could handle that at the time, so I said maybe in the future.

We talked for thirty minutes on the bench. Then I told her my friend was waiting in the car to go surfing. We hugged and cried more, and then we parted ways. I wondered if I'd ever see her again. Like she said, the ball was in my court, and I wasn't sure what to do with it.

Dave and I drove on Highway 17 through the Santa Cruz Mountains. He always drove fast and jerky on the windy road, and I clenched my jaw as we had near-misses with just about every other car.

We went down to the beach, climbed into our wetsuits, and set out into the water. I barely paid attention to catching any waves. I sat on my board and stared out at the sunset, which was partly masked by the marine layer rolling in for the evening. The night was cold, and I felt alone.

I faced a crossroads—did I want to keep in contact with this woman and develop a close relationship with her? Did I want to risk what I had with my adoptive parents, who I thought would surely feel jealous of the new relationship after all they had given me? Did I want them to feel like I was letting them down?

When I got home, I looked at the red fire truck, which still sat on my shelf. I remembered that, even if my parents were putting up a nice veneer, underlying it all was the fact that they really cared about me, that they really wanted me to be safe and loved.

I decided to push it all down, to suppress my desire to get to know where I came from, so I could keep my adoptive parents happy. I decided they were the ones who deserved my love and my respect. I didn't tell my parents about meeting Penny in the park. After that day, I only called Penny once a year, on my birthday. True to her word, she never reached out unless I reached out to her.

It became even more clear to me the importance of the comfort and safety of the Golden Triangle when I left home for college at the University of San Diego. The place itself was astounding. With white mission-style buildings overlooking the ocean, green lawns on the hilltops, and surf-racked cars everywhere, it seemed like I had hit the jackpot. All the girls looked like they had been in movies, and all the guys looked like professional surfers.

For a couple of years, I felt like I was having the time of my life. I moved to Mission Beach my sophomore year and had guys and girls to party with every day. I hung out with attractive girls, surfed, and still managed to get decent grades.

But now, for the first time since being adopted, I was detached from my home base. I didn't have the manufactured safety that my parents had given me.

In one class at the beginning of the semester, I was stuck in a desk up against the back wall. An overwhelming feeling that I couldn't escape took me over, which built itself into a complete fight-or-flight adrenaline rush until I bolted out of the class. I didn't realize I had had a panic attack until after I got out of there.

A friend from the class came up to me afterward. "What happened, man? Were you just really high?"

"Yeah, I was super high. Couldn't be in there anymore."

In reality, I had stopped smoking pot months earlier, because of how paranoid it made me. I went to see a hypnotherapist and got put on anti-anxiety medication.

But the best medication, I discovered, was booze. I started drinking much more heavily, buoyed by the fact that everyone else around me was doing exactly the same thing. Drinking helped me feel like a big guy with big plans, instead of a kid who was scared and alone in a new place, without my support system. I could walk into a party like I owned the place and strike up a conversation with whoever.

My dad called me one day during my sophomore year and asked if I wanted him to ship down the red fire truck, among other items. I told him I was okay. I was forging a different path down here, and it would still be there every time I came back home.

# CHAPTER

## FIVE

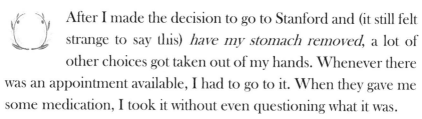 After I made the decision to go to Stanford and (it still felt strange to say this) *have my stomach removed*, a lot of other choices got taken out of my hands. Whenever there was an appointment available, I had to go to it. When they gave me some medication, I took it without even questioning what it was.

But there was one thing I did know: I didn't want to die on my thirty-eighth birthday. So, when a nurse told me my surgery was set for January 30, I asked if we could push it off by a week. She initially looked at me as if to say: *Are you serious? You think you're in the condition to be making this kind of request?* But they were accommodating, and we changed the date to February 6.

I tried going back into work to keep my mind off the calendar, but everyone treated me like a sick puppy that needed to go to his last vet appointment. After a few days, my boss advised me to work from home for my own sake, though I was sure she actually did it for everyone else. I couldn't focus at home, though, as Jen continued to make phone calls and arrange the logistical plans for my treatments.

With two weeks left until the surgery, I was left there to sit and think about everything. *How am I going to eat without a stomach? Am I going to have to give up wine? Do those questions even matter—am I going to die on the operating table?* Jen was there for me, in her own way, but she couldn't really see exactly what I was going through. I started to get lonely and depressed.

Lo and behold, through another one of her connections, Jen heard about a friend of a friend named P.J. Gallaway. Word was that he'd survived a similar surgery to the one I was having.

Similar was an understatement. He had been diagnosed with the same cancer at the same stage as me, just a few months before me, when we were both the same age. Not only that, but he had gone to the same surgeons and gotten the same procedure done, three months ahead of me. He was the spitting image of me as a cancer patient. I'm extremely superstitious, and to me, this didn't feel like a coincidence.

"Do you want to go meet him and his wife down in Redwood City?" Jen asked.

"I mean, yeah. I've got to know what it's going to be like. But what if he looks really shitty?"

"Yeah, I understand. It's up to you."

We decided to make the trip, and a week before the surgery, Jen and I drove down to the Gallaways' house, a small, tan cottage in the suburbs near where I grew up. P.J and his wife, Nancy, both greeted us at the door. Nancy had circles around her eyes and looked weary, but P.J., who was tall and lanky with glasses, wore a beaming smile.

"You must be Steve and Jen," he said. He was dressed in a tucked-in button-down shirt and khakis. "Please, come on in."

The front room was filled with crucifixes and cross-stitches with Bible quotes. I worried that I wasn't going to leave without being baptized. We walked into the living room, and Jen and I sat on a leather couch opposite the other couple.

"This is a really nice home you have," I said.

"It's small, but who can afford anything bigger around here?" Nancy said.

"Mmhmm," I said.

"So," P.J. interjected, "you must have a lot of questions."

"My god, so many. I don't even know where to start. What did you do to prepare for the surgery?"

"Oh, not too much. I mostly just tried to stay positive about it."

"He's underselling himself," Nancy said, patting him and smiling. "He really has been very good. Cut out most of the meat in his diet, no alcohol or anything."

Jen and I glanced at each other.

"Mmhmm, mmhmm," P.J. said, looking pensive. All of a sudden, in a burst of energy, he asked, "Do you want to see my scar?"

I didn't even have time to respond before he started lifting his shirt up to his navel. I almost flinched at the sight, but I caught myself. The skin around his lower torso hung loose, like he had lost a lot of weight very quickly. A raised scar streaked halfway across the left side of his ribcage. *Oh god, is this what I'm going to look like? Is Jen ever going to want to see me naked?* I looked over at her. She had a fake smile plastered on her face.

"It's pretty amazing," P.J. said, tracing his finger along the scar. "This is the only incision they had to make to take out my stomach and a piece of my esophagus. I don't even understand how it all fit out of there."

He talked about the logistics of the surgery, about how he ate without a stomach, and how long the recovery would take.

I sat, halfway listening, trying to muster up the courage to ask the one question I needed to know and at the same time didn't want to know at all.

"What's been the worst part of it?" I finally asked.

The big smile disappeared from his face, and he seemed to retreat inside himself. The energy was sucked out of the room.

I almost apologized for asking, when a coy smile sprang across his face. He looked at his wife, then back at me.

"Without a doubt, it has got to be my gas. It comes at all hours, without warning. It almost peels the paint off the walls."

We sat silent for a second, and then I couldn't help it. I keeled over laughing. I laughed harder than I had in months. PJ joined in, followed by Jen and Nancy, and we all sat in the living room cracking up together, four strangers bonded together by a disease. Right in that moment, I felt so much of my fear shed from my body like a dense coat. I could still laugh. I could still smile, and maybe, just maybe, I could get through this.

As we said our goodbyes, I thanked P.J. and thought that as long as he stayed alive, I would be okay. P.J. wasn't lying in bed with cables flowing out of his body mumbling requests for Jell-O or euthanasia. He mostly just seemed like a normal guy, except for a scar, some loose skin, and some horrible gas.

"I feel so relieved," I said to Jen in the car.

"Good, I'm glad," she replied, her hands gripped tight on the steering wheel.

"Like, I was skeptical when I saw the 35 crosses in the living room, but I think this is a guy whose number I'm glad to have in my phone."

Jen stayed silent for several seconds. "Did you notice his wife?" she finally asked.

"Yeah, she seemed like she's really handling it well. Seems really supportive."

"I thought she just looked so, I don't know, *tired.*"

"Hm, yeah, I guess she did look a little tired."

"Yeah."

We were silent for most of the drive home. Jen kept her head glued forward, hands at ten and two, eyes on the road, while I looked out the window at the rolling green fields as we headed north.

\* \* \*

The days, filled with an inability to show attention to the usual aspects of life, given how much life was about to change, slowly rolled by. I knew just about everything there was to know about the surgery and recovery process. There was only one piece of information I didn't research: the post-op survival rate from the cancer. I didn't want to know, to be defined by a percentage. Jen never mentioned whether or not she ever looked it up, either.

In the few days before the surgery, it became less abstract just how much my life was about to change. When I cooked spaghetti with meat sauce, I wondered if it would be the last time I'd ever be able to eat that. When I bought a new wine bottle to put in my rapidly-filling cellar, I wondered if the whole thing would just be for show from there on out. And when I kissed Mia goodnight, I wondered if she would ever really know her father. I spent a few extra minutes at her crib at night looking at her and cooing to her. Sometimes she looked back at me, and sometimes she just slept.

The doctors told me I would have to fast for 24 hours before the surgery. Of course, I wanted to go out with a bang. Several of my oldest friends came in from around California the night before I had to drive down to Stanford. Before we went out, I went down to the wine cellar to grab a bottle for dinner. My eyes glossed over the Opus One cabernet, the five-hundred dollar vintage I had bought years earlier. That was the bottle I was saving for when we hosted an ambassador at our house or something. But as I kept scanning the shelf, my mind stayed on that bottle.

*You might die on the operating table. When's a better time to drink this than right now?*

I grabbed the bottle and set out to meet my friends at a Brazilian steakhouse in San Francisco called Boboquivari's. I struggled to eat a filet mignon, but finished the entire thing, powered by the resolve that I was going to ENJOY my last meal, dammit. I washed every bite down with the Opus One.

"Impressive work, Melen," said Buddy, one of my oldest friends from the Golden Triangle. "When they take that stomach out of you, it's gonna weigh fifteen pounds."

I laughed. "They'll definitely need some heavy machinery to get it out."

We talked and laughed like nothing was going on, like we were all still in college together, and no time had passed. But I could sense an undercurrent among my friends. They were nervous. I was nervous. Why couldn't we talk about it?

"I'm really scared," I finally said, one of the first times I had admitted a feeling that had been percolating in the back of my mind for weeks. Jen took my hand underneath the table. "But I'm so grateful for all of you. I love my life and I can't tell you what this means to me. I don't know what's going to happen, but I'm going to do everything possible to make it through this."

The table was silent. I paused to wipe away the tears gathering on my face. I saw my friends wiping tears away, too. I wasn't sure if they were all just sympathizing with me, or if they were thinking that the next time they'd all be together, it would be at my funeral.

The rest of that night, we ate, drank, and inhaled everything in sight. I probably would have done crack if it was in front of me at the time. Late at night, four friends and I went back to my house and stood in the wine cellar for hours, drinking and reminiscing nearly until the sun rose.

Rick, my freshman year roommate, was sitting on the floor of the cellar, leaning against one of the wine racks, when he started to choke up.

"I know when we all get together, we can just go right into having a good time without talking too much about the serious stuff. But I want you guys to know I love you all."

We hugged and cried, then laughed some more. I went to bed when the sun rose and slept in, a dreamless drunken doze that left me in the morning feeling like I never slept at all.

I woke up a bit woozy , feeling like a walking mistake on the day I was set to check into the hospital.

We dropped Mia off at Jen's parents' place. Jen drove us down to Palo Alto as I sat in the passenger seat with my throbbing head against the window.

"I told you this was going to happen when you were on your second glass," she said.

"Maybe cut me some slack? How am I supposed to act right now?"

She sped down Highway 280. An hour later, we checked into the hotel in Palo Alto.

Jen and I settled in our room for the evening. *Twelve hours to go.* I ate a banana and sat on the bed, while Jen washed her face. The room was empty, silent, a blank slate far away from everything I had known, everything that could comfort me.

"Jen. What's going to happen if I don't make it?"

She turned the faucet off and turned around.

"Don't say that. It isn't going to happen."

"But, Jen," I said, tears welling up in my eyes. "It could. What are you and Mia going to do? What would you tell Mia about me?"

She sat on the bed next to me. "You have to stay strong, Steve. It's going to work. You met PJ. We've got the best doctors in the world."

"I'm just so scared. What if they put me under and I never wake up? I didn't say goodbye to Mia. I should have written her a letter. I should have —"

She pulled me in and hugged me, and I cried on her shoulder.

We spent the rest of the night watching movies in bed. I withdrew from my thoughts and fell asleep in the middle of *a random HBO movie.*

The next morning, we got up before sunrise and headed to Stanford. As I walked down the misty tree-lined campus paths to the hospital, the Bay Area fog seemed to penetrate every pore of my skin all the way into my core. I was acutely aware of the soppy texture of the moisture coating my arm. With each inhale, I could sense the ever-so-slight heaviness of the tiny water droplets suspended in the atmosphere going into my chest. Suddenly, for a brief moment, my mind was clear before the whirlwind of what was about to happen to me came rushing back.

*Is this what it takes to finally live in the moment? Do I have to go into a life-or-death surgery to appreciate life?*

Within a minute, a small muscular Filipino guy who still looked like he was in medical school came to fetch me and Jen.

He took out a needle to get my bloodwork, then pricked me once in the arm. He apologized, explaining he missed the vein, and tried again unsuccessfully. He pricked me four more times before the syringe finally filled up with blood. Whatever confidence I had was officially checked. A wave of superstition took me over. If this guy couldn't even do the simplest thing in medicine, could I trust someone to take out my stomach and sew my esophagus to my intestine? Was I about to make a huge mistake?

A nurse gave me stacks of paperwork to fill out before the seven-hour-long surgery. On one page, I saw a new vocabulary word: "splenectomy."

"What? Splenectomy?" I asked the nurse.

"We need you to sign that in case they find out it's necessary during the surgery," the nurse responded.

"Find out what is necessary?"

"The splenectomy."

"Which is ... what?"

"Removing your spleen."

Jen stood up. "You didn't want to tell us about this before?"

"Ma'am, unexpected things can happen in surgeries. We need to have this paperwork in case we find something while we're in there."

I signed off on the paperwork—what else was I supposed to do?—and off the nurse went to let the superiors know that it was ok to dig out more of my organs.

Another nurse came in and said she needed to shave my chest. Ridiculously, I started to think about lying naked on that operating table. Maybe I should've trimmed downstairs beforehand?

*Oh, well, too late now.*

While she was shaving me, Dr. N came into the room. He was wearing scrubs instead of his lab coat and bifocals that sat low on his nose.

"How are you doing, Steve?"

"Oh. Hanging in there." I was distracted by the nurse shaving dangerously close to my nipple.

"Well, it's almost time to head into the OR. Are you ready?"

"Not sure I'll ever be ready. But let's do it."

He called in a group of assistants, who unlocked my bed as the nurse finished.

Jen took my hand and held it tight for a few seconds. "I'll be right out here when you're done."

They started to roll my bed, which resisted with a squeak before sliding across the tile floor. I gave Jen a thumbs up as I was wheeled away.

"See ya on the other side," I said. She frowned, and I immediately regretted my limp attempt at a joke. *Was this going to be the last thing I said to her?* "I love you, Jen," I said, unsure if Jen could hear me, as they pushed me through the double doors. We passed by a number of rooms bustling with activity. People were moving everywhere around us and I started to panic. This was really about to happen.

The nurse pushed me into another blank white room that looked exactly like a scene from the TV show *ER*. Three doctors came inside and surrounded me, babbling medical terms. The anesthesiologist told me to count down from ten.

This was it. A roll of the dice.

"Okay. Ten ..."

*This all happened so fast. Are they sure they measured everything right?*

"Nine ..."

*Should I have called my biological mom and told her I loved her?*

"Eight ..."

*Am I going to die?*

"Seven ..."

# CHAPTER

# SIX

I woke up confused. I was in a blurry, white room, a blue curtain to my right and a wall just a few inches to my left.

A potent smell of disinfectant hit my nose, almost covering an underlying smell like an arm that had been under a cast for months. Beeps and buzzes and a noise like someone breathing in a spacesuit came from somewhere, or maybe everywhere. It all came together to form an orchestra announcing that I wasn't waking up at home, in my king bed, under my 600-thread count sheets.

Something serious just happened to me—*but what?* I blinked and opened my eyes wide. Two people in blue jump suits — no, scrubs — were hovering nearby. One was hanging a bag of clear liquid on a pole near my feet, and the other was scribbling loudly on a chart.

*I'm in the hospital. I just had surgery. Holy shit. I'm alive!*

A tingling sensation spread through my fingers and arms and to my torso. My breathing wasn't normal; it felt like someone was sitting on my chest. I looked down and saw a tube snaking its way from my neck to one of about a dozen monitors at my bedside. I reached my hand up and felt it, tracing upwards, until the line ended at my nose.

The nurse, a short, thin woman with boyish black hair, noticed.

"I see you've found your NG tube," she said. She had a kind, motherly voice that didn't match her young appearance. "How do you feel?"

The first words came out hoarse. "Tight. My body feels tight. And everything feels ... a little confused. What all happened?"

"We can get a surgeon in here to explain in more detail," she said. The second nurse opened the curtain at the foot of my bed and left.

"How long have I been out?" I would have believed her if she told me it was a minute or if she said it was a week.

"It was about seven hours all in all. You did great in there. Your wife is waiting outside. Do you want to see her?"

I thought for a second. *What do I even look like right now?* "Maybe in a minute. Can I see myself?"

"Sure." She handed me a mirror, and I slowly brought it up to my face. I looked like shit. My cheeks were hollow, sunken in, and dark bags circled the bottoms of my eyes. My skin looked a pale shade of yellow well beyond my pallid color when I went to Palm Springs. Inside the NG tube, a few inches below my nose, was a clump of brown fluid like swamp goo. I wondered if the goo was going into my body or coming out of it. Suddenly, answering my question, another clump of the gunk shot out of my nose, pushing the first clump down the tube toward the end of my bed. I gagged at the sight and lowered the mirror.

The nurse smiled. "It's normal drainage from the surgery. Might look a little gross, but it's nothing to be worried about."

"Are you, like, my assigned nurse?"

She laughed. "Well, I have to sleep sometimes. But I'll be in and out of here, yes. I'm Maria."

I tried to raise my hand to shake hers, but my strength failed.

Maria looked at me apologetically. "Oh, no need. You just get as much rest as you need."

I nodded weakly and shifted my attention to my body, which was covered by a blanket. After hesitating for a second, I lifted the sheet and stared in awe. Long tubes seemed to flow everywhere, concentrating into a mass of tangled cords on my chest. Clear liquid flowed up into one tube attached to my arm, while some other fluid seemed to come out of my right oblique. A long bandage was stuck like bubblegum to my abdomen around my left side and over to my back. My feet were supported by two metal extenders hanging off the end of the bed.

For a long time, I lay motionless, in a sort of trance, completely transfixed by what I barely recognized as my own body. It just looked like a heap of human flesh. Someone else's flesh.

"Is it weird that I don't really feel anything right now?"

"Not at all," Maria said as she wrote down numbers from a monitor. "We gave you some painkillers just a bit ago."

The curtain jerked back, and Dr. S's face appeared.

"Hello, Steve."

"Don't get too many Scandinavians in here, do you?" I asked, pointing to the foot extenders at the end of the bed.

"Oh, I don't know about that," he said. He took a look at my chart and then at me, his mouth curving into a quick smile before settling back to a straight face. "The surgery went well," he said, with a little bit less enthusiasm than I needed. While Dr. N was always the loudest person in the room, with a booming laugh and an in-your-face confidence, Dr. S was quieter, more cerebral.

He continued, "We took out your whole stomach, as expected, and we had to take out a part of your esophagus and your spleen to be careful. While we were in there, we also found more than a dozen lymph nodes behind your pancreas that were swollen. So, we had no choice but to take out half of your pancreas."

Jesus, how many parts of my body could these guys take out? "What? I mean, what does my pancreas do? Can I live with half of it?"

"Your pancreas helps break down food through your intestines."

I waited for him to continue, but he stood looking at my chart.

"And, do I need that?"

"You should be just fine," he said, looking up. "You've got a long road ahead of you, but you've been doing well so far. How much pain are you in?"

"I don't feel much. I'm just a little ... tight is the way I guess I'd describe it."

"Mm. You'll probably be going through some pain over the next few weeks. To conduct the surgery, we had to induce fractures on four of your ribs."

"You broke my ribs?"

"Yes. And your body will likely be going through other changes, as well. Since we took out your stomach, your other organs will likely shift to occupy that space."

"My organs are going to *move?* Am I going to feel that?"

"You might. What we did in the surgery is connect your esophagus directly to your small intestine. It's going to be a healing process as your body gets used to it. But within a few weeks, you should be close to normal."

He paused for a few seconds, as if expecting me to ask something.

"The only thing you have to do now, Steve, is recover," Dr. S said, and he left the room.

I sat there looking up at the ceiling, wondering if I would be able to *feel* the emptiness in my body. But I couldn't. Why would it be so noticeable if my hand got chopped off, but not when a whole organ is gone from my body? Is it literally just because I can't see it?

*Maybe I need to start doing some yoga, get in touch with my inner self or whatever.*

It hit me that while everything before was abstract — *I'm going to have surgery, I'm going to get my stomach removed* — it was now concrete. I now had to live the rest of my life without a stomach. The feeling weighed me down as it truly sunk in that my life was never going to be the same.

For a minute, I cried alone in bed, until the nurse told me Jen was asking to come in.

"Okay, send her in," I said, trying to pull myself together.

Her eyes were puffy, and she wore a smile that had obviously been set into place the second before she got in the door. I could tell she had been going through hell. *God, what have I put her through? What am I still putting her through? She didn't buy into this. She doesn't deserve this, me, for a husband.*

She looked at me from a few feet away, then came toward me and took my hand. She held it lightly, like she didn't know what to do with it. Like if she jerked it too hard one of the tubes would come out or my skinny wrist would snap in half.

"How—how do you feel?" she asked.

"Never better," I said, with a short laugh. "Now comes the easy part."

I was trying to comfort her, to make things light, but she didn't smile. Right on cue, another shot of brown goop came out of my nose. Jen flinched but regained her composure quickly.

"Don't worry, the nurse said that's normal," I said.

"I knew you were going to make it. I knew the whole time I was out there that you'd be okay."

I looked at her but didn't say anything.

"You look really good," she said.

I smiled. "You liar."

She smiled back. "No, I'm serious. I thought you would look worse."

I didn't really believe her, but a part of me also needed to hear that. I needed to know not just that I was going to survive, but that I wouldn't come out of here a freak.

"Do you want me to flip on the TV?" she asked.

"Sure."

She picked up the remote and pushed a button. Some small-court claims judge show was on, which told me it must be mid-afternoon. Jen pulled her chair back parallel to mine, and we watched TV for the next few hours. Doctors came in and out, taking readings, injecting new things into my body, pushing buttons on monitors.

I felt numb, and I settled into the fact that this would be my life for the next week.

"I miss Mia," I said.

She looked at me. "Do you want me to bring her down next time?"

"No. I mean, I miss her, and I know seeing her would cheer me up. But I don't want her to see me like this. I don't want to leave a scar on her, of seeing her daddy with tubes coming out of his body."

"She'll be happy to see you either way."

"I know. I know."

We looked at each other for a few seconds, at a loss for words.

Sometime later, a college friend named Buddy came in. We had met on our first day of college and gone surfing together in Mission Beach. Years later, we were in each other's weddings.

He looked tired, which told me that it must have been nighttime. Time had no real meaning to me anymore as I spent every minute under a white fluorescent bulb.

"Steve," he said, more quietly than I'd ever heard him say anything. People talked in hushed voices in here, and I could never entirely figure out why. "How do you feel?"

"A little delirious. But I'm hanging in there."

Buddy, Jen, and I sat by the TV, the passing hours indicated by the dull hum of the trashy tabloid shows replaced by trashy cop shows. Boredom set in, and I started to feel guilty about how much time they were giving up just to sit here.

At one point in the night, we heard from a gossipy nurse that Patrick Swayze was getting treated right at that moment in a nearby room for pancreatic cancer. Obviously, we weren't going to try to meet him, but it was something to talk about. Leaning low in his chair with his feet kicked up on my bed, Buddy started reading an article about it.

"Apparently, he was filming a pilot episode for a show called *The Beast* when he started getting a burning feeling in his stomach," Buddy said.

*Sounds like China,* I thought.

"Then, three weeks later, he got diagnosed with Stage IV pancreatic cancer."

"One stage worse than me. At least I'm not that bad off."

"It says: 'He travelled to Stanford University Medical Center to have surgery to remove intra-, intra-ductal, papillary, muck-, mucinous, ne-o-plaz, neoplasms.' Hey Melen, think you can spell 'intraductal papillary mucinous neoplasms?'"

"E-N..."

"Nope."

"Didn't anyone ever tell you not to quiz someone with more than five tubes coming out of their body?"

"Nope, never heard that one."

"Keep reading the article, asshat."

He laughed. "Now, at Stanford, the whole hospital is in a state of frenzy as Swayze is treated on the same floor as the one-and-only, the incomparable, USD Class of '92 *cum laude* graduate Steve Melen—"

I laughed. "Yeah, all the women in here keep asking me to pull down my pants."

Jen shot me a glare as Buddy doubled over in his chair. I wanted to laugh with him, but it hurt.

All of a sudden, a massive wad of green and black liquid shot out of my nose down the NG tube. It was much bigger than anything that had come out up to that point. A monitor started beeping furiously at my bedside. Buddy went white. Jen's eyes looked like they were about to pop out of her head.

"What the hell was that?" I asked.

"I—I don't know," Buddy said, sounding like he was trying to keep his voice steady. He gulped. "Are you okay?"

"I don't know. I feel kind of lightheaded."

"I'll go get someone," he said, already halfway out of his chair.

A wave of total exhaustion came over my body. I felt numb. The walls of the room started going blurry. I couldn't control my breathing and felt my heartbeat in my skull.

Jen's face appeared above me.

"Steve, what's wrong? What's wrong?" She was frantic.

"Don't panic, Jen. We're going to — we're going to —"

Within seconds, Buddy was back with Maria, the nurse.

"Steve, I need you to stay with me," Maria said.

"Okay, okay —" My head was spinning. I struggled to keep my eyes open. I felt myself going in and out of consciousness. "I don't know what's wrong with me."

Buddy ran out of the room, looking like he was about to vomit, while a rush of other people came in. A lot of indecipherable, nervous chatter floated around. The cacophony of their voices heightened my fear.

"...Normal drainage," said a man.

I saw Maria step to the front. "I've been monitoring ..." It faded out and back in. "...seriously wrong."

Louder and louder—an argument. Jen's voice came at a distance. I just wanted everyone to stop yelling. I just wanted to sleep. I just...

Maria's voice came loud out of the clamor: "Code Blue, Room 112. Room 112. Code Blue, Room 112."

A rush of doctors, and my world became a tiny circle of white lab coats. A needle appeared directly under my eyes. *Are they drugging me?* A flash of the film *Twelve Monkeys* inexplicably came to my mind. I thought I was being taken to a mental hospital.

"What's going on?" I asked. "Something's not right. I don't know, I don't know."

"Take him to the OR..." a voice said.

"Emergency surgery..." said another, or maybe the same one. All the voices were on a delay from the movement of mouths.

Jen was yelling in the background.

"Whaddareyou ...what's going on?" I tried.

A blur of faceless people detached what cables they could as a team of four started rolling me out of the room.

The white hospital light hit my eyes. My vision focused for a second. I tried to sit up, but four lab coats held me down.

"It's *Twelve Monkeys*!" I yelled. "It's just like *Twelve Monkeys*! It's *Twelve Monkeys*!"

"Where's the sedation?" someone yelled.

The ceiling of the hospital rushed by my eyes as the doctors ran, pushing me toward the elevator.

I yelled, "Stop! Stop! I don't want to die!"

Someone pushed the button on the elevator a dozen times until it opened. They shoved me in head-first, but the door wouldn't close. The foot extenders were too long.

"Break it off!" someone yelled.

I heard a *pound, pound, pound,* kicking the extenders off my bed. Jen's worried face was just on the other side of the elevator, blurring in and out of focus, as I issued my last hallucinatory warning.

"Jennifer! It's *Twelve Monkeys!*"

Finally, a *thwack* sounded in the hallway as the extenders gave. The elevator door closed, and I passed out.

I wouldn't wake back up for another four days.

\* \* \*

The whirring blades of a helicopter thumped against the window to my room, jolting me awake. The doctors' bodies and faces were all shadowed except for the blinding white lab coats. They were making final preparations just on the other side of the door. This cabal had taken my organs out and was loading them into a cooler to ship off to China. It was only a matter of time before they got to their most prized pieces—my heart, my lungs, my liver. I wasn't sure how I knew. I just knew.

Another pair of shadows, speaking in whispers, hovered inside the room. These were the people they were trying to pass off as nurses, but I wasn't fooled.

It was dark except for the green and red lights flashing on and off. In the corner of my vision, I saw Jennifer sitting, on her phone, completely unaware of what was about to happen. I knew I needed to make my move, and soon.

Finally, a command came from the outside, and the nurses left the room. I had my chance. I darted my eyes over to Jen and grabbed her wrist, hard.

"Jen, we've got to get out of here. They're taking me on a ship out to the bay."

She looked at me in horror, opening her mouth then closing it. *Good, she understands. But why isn't she moving? Go, go, take your chance now before they get you.*

"We've got to get the fuck out of here!"

Jen stayed frozen in her chair for a second but then launched up. I tried to jump out of bed but was held back by cables and wires.

"Nuuuuuuurse!" she screamed.

*You fucking traitor.*

All of a sudden, two of the shadow-nurses and a lab coat came running into the room.

*This is it, my last chance.*

I grabbed the tube in my arm and tried to pull, but the white coat latched onto my wrist and pinned it to the side of the bed.

"Sedation!" he called.

"No, no, no! Fuck you! You can't do this!"

The shadow-nurse raised the needle, which glimmered from a distant light and dripped with a thick serum. I gave everything, struggling against the man's strength. It wasn't enough.

She brought the needle down into my IV, and I knew this was it, this was the end, and Jen would regret everything she had just done when she realized...

\* \* \*

It was still dark the next time I woke up, the room lit only by the monitors near my head and a distant hallway light. I tried to move my arm but it held tight. The other one moved an inch before holding fast. The same for both of my legs. I was strapped down. I tried to tilt my head up, but the pain in my abdomen forced me back down. I groaned.

A small, older nurse who I didn't recognize was sitting across from my bed. She tensed up, putting her hands on the arms of the chair like she was ready to launch.

"What the fuck is going on here?" I said, struggling with my wrists against the straps.

She stayed seated. "You were in psychosis. A couple of days ago, you tried to rip all of your cords out, so we had to tie you down."

Suddenly it all came back to me—the doctors, the helicopter. That was *days* ago?

"Why would that happen?"

"We call it ICU psychosis. Some people get it when they've been sedated for long periods of time."

I felt ashamed. How could this sweet woman be part of a grand conspiracy to steal my organs? Who would want my organs at this point, anyway? Clearly these are the bargain-bin organs.

But also: Why the fuck were there thousands of spiders crawling out of the ceiling above her?

"I'm sorry, but do you see that?" I said, motioning behind her with my head.

She turned around, bewildered.

"There's, like, a thousand spiders on the wall behind you. I mean, not like spider-spiders I guess. Like ghost spiders."

"Ghost spiders?"

"Yeah, they're kind of translucent."

"Hm."

She walked out of the room without a word. I stared at the corner of the ceiling as waves of spiders seemed to crawl out and expand in a circle, then retract on themselves. They seemed to be in constant motion but never moving anywhere.

The light clicked on in the room, and in walked a newer friend, Rider Rowen, wearing a white lab coat. The short nurse followed him. Under the light, the spiders disappeared, and the ceiling was just the ceiling.

"Rider? What are you doing here?"

"I work here, Steve."

"Oh, right." He was an anesthesiologist at Stanford.

"If I take the straps off your arms and legs, are you going to try to rip your IVs out and strangle me?"

"Well, a second ago I saw a thousand spiders crawling out of the ceiling, but no. Rider is friend, not enemy."

He smiled and nodded to the nurse. She started with the straps around my ankles, then did my wrists. I flexed my hands and feet. They felt weak. A fuzzy static went through my limbs as blood starting to flow freely.

Rider sat down, which comforted me. All the doctors had been constantly standing, moving, pushing, injecting, and finally someone would just sit and talk.

"How long have I been out?" I asked.

"It's been seven days since you started crashing. You've been in a medically-induced coma."

I was stunned into silence. A whole week of my life, vanished into oblivion. I tried to think if I could remember anything from those seven days. But no. It didn't feel any different from a regular night of sleep.

"A— a week?" I finally stammered.

"We had to keep you sedated to be sure that the new connection we made would hold."

"What connection?"

He recounted what had happened that night. Apparently, after Buddy ran out of the room, the on-call doctor came in with the nurse, Maria. The doctor thought it was all normal from the procedure, but Maria had been with me the whole time and knew something wasn't right. She went over his head and called a Code

Blue on the intercom, telling all the staff that I was crashing. She saved my life.

"We took you to the OR and opened you up on the spot," Rider said. "I was your anesthesiologist for the surgery. We found that the connection between your esophagus and your small intestine had sprung a leak. It was spewing out blood and bile into your body, and it almost put you into sepsis."

He paused and sighed into his hands.

"I was in charge of monitoring your vitals. Two times, I was ready to go outside and tell Jen that you weren't going to make it. It was all over." He choked back tears. "I was really scared we were going to lose you."

"I — I don't even know what to say."

"You're lucky you're here. These surgeons are incredible. They used this mesh device to wrap around the connection and keep everything contained. I don't know how they kept you from going into sepsis, but they did. They sewed you back up and put you in a coma to make sure it would all hold together."

"Wow." I sat in disbelief. I had come so close to dying. Was I *still* in danger? "How much longer am I going to have to be here?"

"It's hard to say right now, Steve. At least another few weeks."

"Weeks?" I said. "I thought I was supposed to be starting chemo."

"You have to know how serious this thing is that happened to you. We aren't even entirely sure how well the new connection will hold. We're in uncharted territory here, and we can't have something catastrophic happen while you're at home."

"Is Jen here?" I asked.

"Not right now. She had to go home to take care of your baby. But she has been driving here every day, spending hours with you. Your uncle has been here every day too."

"Do you think I'm going to be okay, Rider?"

He stared at me for a long time. He had a tendency to drift into long silences, churning in his head.

"As your friend, I want to say yes. But the real answer is that I don't know." He paused. "I want to suggest something for you. I think you should write a letter to your daughter. Tell her how you feel about her. Tell her what you are like and what you hope for her. Tell her you love her."

"Rider..." I trailed off.

"Just think about it, Steve. I've got to get back to my shift. I'll call Jen and let her know you're awake."

After he left, I sat in bed and cried. What if it happened again, while I was here alone? Would I die with no one here to hold my hand?

I thought about what he said, about writing a letter to Mia. But I just couldn't do it. If I did that, it would feel like I was giving up, like I could be complete with my life and just go off quietly into the night. But I didn't want to die for her. I wanted to *live* for her. I wanted to see her grow up. I wanted to hear her first words, and see her personality, how she was like me, how she was nothing like me. I couldn't say goodbye.

I sat in the bed alone for a long time, with the sound of the beeping monitors at my bedside as the only thing to keep me present to where I was, to just how much I had gone through, to how much further I still had to go.

# CHAPTER
# SEVEN

 It's not hard to tell how bad a hospital patient is doing at any given time: just look at how many monitors they have attached to them. After my second surgery, I was transferred over to a real room with an actual window — an indicator it was going to be a long ride—and hooked up to about a dozen different beeping, flashing, injecting and inflating machines. Two IVs came out of my arms, connecting to a bag hung on a rolling rack, giving me all the nutrients I would need to survive. The NG tube, which the doctors told me went all the way from my nose to my intestine, drained to another boxy machine near my head. And a set of electrodes gathered near my heart, pumping out data to the EKG machine attached to the wall.

It was all extremely anxiety-provoking. Over 20 minutes, I got used to the steady beep ... beep ... beep emitting from my right ear, until out of the blue I heard beep ... BEEPBEEP ... beep. *Oh fuck I'm dying!*

Jen was even more undone by nerves than I was, careening out of her chair to the nurse's station whenever a beep sounded particularly ominous or a bag hung empty on the rack. After a few days, I started to feel anxious every time she came in the room. It was different, being together again without our daughter. I wanted to see Mia so bad, but at this point she probably wouldn't have even recognized me.

"So, I looked up the things you'll be able to eat when you get out of here," Jen said, the day after I woke up from my coma. "I think you'll be able to eat a lot of different things! Mostly soft foods, nothing too greasy or spicy. But I've got a grocery list going."

"Jen, it's going to be another *three weeks* that I'm in here. I can't even think ahead to tomorrow, let alone that far."

"I know, I know. But when we get there, I'm just trying to say, I think it will all be okay."

How could she be thinking three weeks ahead of now, when we weren't even sure I was going to make it out of the hospital alive? I was still convinced, even though everyone had assured me otherwise, that I was going to die.

Right on cue, the sound of someone screaming down the hallway erupted. We both sat in silence listening. *Is this going to be me?*

Sure enough, when the pain medication wore off, I could feel a rising, throbbing pain envelop my whole body. It started with a tingle in my fingers and toes, then continued with aches traveling up my arms and legs and finally, peaking to an all-encompassing pain like being stabbed a thousand times throughout my torso.

I moaned and yelled until a nurse came in and gave me an injection and within minutes my body went numb in the reverse order: first in my torso, then down to my arms, and finally ending at my fingers and toes. I felt light, like I could just float out of my bed if it weren't so damn comfortable.

At 5 a.m. on my second day, a team of doctors walked into my room and flipped on the harsh white light to assess me.

"We are going to be helping you manage your pain," the tallest of the doctors said. The group was all on the younger side, the type of people who seemed like they could be on *Gray's Anatomy* or something. "How are you feeling today?"

"Mostly groggy right now. My throat hurts, and my left side feels really tight."

"How would you rate your pain on a level of one to ten?"

I looked over at the wall, where a poster with a range of smiling to frowning faces showed a spectrum of pain. Under the Zero, the cartoon face looked like it was spending a day at the spa. At Ten, the face looked like someone must be pulling out its teeth with a pair of pliers.

"Um. A six?"

"Mm. Mmhmm." They nodded and looked at each other importantly, then huddled in the far corner of the room. "Today we are going to prescribe you two doses of Lortab and Oxycodone. Additionally, you'll notice this little control pad attached to your bed. The tall doctor pulled up a wired controller that looked like a TV remote with just one big, green button. "Once the pad lights up, you can push the green button and be administered a dose of Dilaudid."

I had no idea what any of the things they said were, but I didn't really care. *Fuck it, just give me everything,* I thought, which I'm not sure was all that far off from what they were thinking, too.

The green button lit up every fifteen minutes. I pushed it the moment I saw that light, every time. The first few times, I only felt a slight, creeping pain by minute fifteen, but soon I was writhing in pain within ten minutes, staring at the button until it lit up. It eventually became the only thing I looked forward to, as I experienced a visceral, soothing sensation every time the button lit up. I was Pavlov's dog, drooling for my pain meds.

\* \* \*

While I was under sedation, they put a catheter inside me. I was shocked to learn that there was one still in me when I was awake, thinking that I would *feel* a tube stuck all the way up my pee-hole.

One morning, a male nurse told me to try to pee.

"Just like I normally would?"

"Yes. Exactly."

I looked at the catheter and hesitated. It looked kinked like a garden hose. It didn't take much brain power to think of what that could mean.

"I don't know. It looks like it's twisted," I said, pointing at the tube.

"It's fine," he replied without looking.

Not wanting to question things further, I took a deep breath in and struggled for a few seconds, almost forgetting how to pee. Suddenly, an intense burn started at the end of my pee hole and traveled in an inferno up my pelvis and into my abdomen, as if my pee were lighter fluid and someone had just lit a match.

"Fuuuuuuck! Fuck!" I screamed.

"Oh, shit! Okay, hold on." He rushed out of the chair to get the head nurse.

"You said it was okay!" I screamed at him as he ran out the door. "You said it was fucking *okay,* you son of a bitch!"

Another nurse, a woman this time, rushed in and pulled the catheter out. What I had imagined would be the worst part of having a catheter ended up being the best, as a wave of relief flowed over me when she removed it.

I breathed deeply, shivering with anger as the pain slowly receded away.

"How much pain did you feel?" she asked.

"A ten! A ten out of ten! A goddamn twenty! God damn that nurse! I knew it was messed up!"

She looked sympathetic and wrote something on her chart. "Let's get you over to the bathroom."

"I haven't even stood up yet." Tears were falling down my face. "I'll help you."

She removed the IVs from my arms and detached the electrodes from my chest. She kicked the wheels on the three machines still attached to me and rolled them over to my bedside, then grabbed my arm to help me up. The ground chilled my feet even in socks. When I tried to stand, my legs nearly gave way. I hobbled in a hunch over to the bathroom, moving an inch at a time as I cried and howled for the male nurse's head. This was not how I imagined reaching my first milestone after surgery would go.

* * *

The next several days were an exercise of constant discomfort. All day and all night—both of which were indistinguishable anyway—people came in and out of my room. Doctors flipped on the lights and introduced themselves, pushed buttons and pricked veins, took measurements and nodded, then left the room never to be seen again.

I even had a fart nurse, a woman whose one job seemed to be coming into my room throughout the day to ask if I had flatulated yet. My answer the first few times was a sheepish *no, thank you for asking.* Judging by her disappointed reaction, this seemed to be the wrong answer. Eventually, it became our little daily tradition.

"Happened yet?" she asked me.

"Nope, but I can't wait to see what kind of cake you get me when it does."

On my fourth day post-coma, a nurse told me I had a visitor. Jen was sitting in the room with me working on her laptop.

Jen looked up. "Are you expecting someone, Steve?"

"No, not right now. Who is it?"

"He said his name was Sandip," the nurse said.

"Huh."

"Who is Sandip?" Jen asked.

"He's one of my clients."

"I don't think you should be seeing a client right now."

I thought for a second. Sandip was an older man and one of my favorite clients. He always radiated kindness and wisdom. But I would never describe him as a close friend.

It hit me how terrible I must look to someone from the outside world. Sure, the nurses and doctors had been intent on inquiring about my farts, but now a client who only knew me from the context of my business was coming to see me in my most vulnerable state. I hadn't had a stomach or a shower in twelve days. My hair looked like a rat's nest, and I knew I smelled.

But still, I wanted to feel like I could talk to someone who wasn't an immediate family member. I wanted to feel like I was still part of life outside of this hospital.

I called for Sandip to be let in. Jen left the room to give us some privacy. While waiting, I finger-combed my hair over to the side and sat up in bed, trying to hold my shoulders high. I gathered the tubes and wires coming out of my body and hid them under the blanket.

Sandip walked in the door and paused for a second, looking at me without saying anything. He smiled and came to my bed. I was completely caught off guard by that smile. I felt accepted in that moment, like someone was seeing through everything about my body and feeling everything I was feeling. He was unafraid.

I realized I had been holding my breath, and I exhaled sharply. Right then, all the emotions that had been stuffed inside exploded out. I burst into uncontrollable tears, sobbing while this man from my prior life stood over my bed. For a brief moment, I thought that I needed to pull myself together, that a client couldn't see me like this, but he only moved closer. I kept crying. I needed to cry.

He put his right hand on my forehead and held it there. It was warm and dry. Suddenly, a strange wave of calm washed over me. For the first time in days, I felt that everything was going to be okay. All the tension, all the anxiety melted away. My breath slowed as the tears stopped flowing.

He took his hand away. I felt like I had been touched by a deity.

"I—I don't know what just happened there," I said. "I was overwhelmed—"

"It's ok, Steve," he said. "I understand."

I was awestruck. I had thought he would be coming to talk with me about his account. I was so stuck in the mindset that he was a *client* that I couldn't fathom the compassion he had toward me. He saw me in pain and did the only thing he could do to help me.

When he left, a sadness took me over. I wondered why everyone else in my life found it so hard to look me in the eyes and just see me and what I was going through. They all seemed to be filtering my experience through their own fears of death. In thirty seconds, Sandip saw me in a way no one else had seen me. After that, every time I felt a crushing, devastating wave of anxiety, of feeling like I can't make it through all this, I thought about the man who saw me in pain and did whatever he could to help me heal.

* * *

Days later, I felt like I could get out of bed and walk around. With the help of two nurses, I pulled my tubes and wires over the side and placed one toe on the ground at a time. I held on to the bed handles to make sure that my feet could still hold me.

I walked hunched out of my room and to the nurse's station, dragging my heels along the floor as my head started spinning from suddenly being vertical. I carried with me an IV pole and a rolling cart that had several monitors attached. I looked around the area, sneaking peeks into other patients' rooms. Some had four monitors.

Some had one or two. None of them were the walking supercomputer that was Steve Melen.

But things continued to get better, little by little. An on-call doctor eventually came in to take out the NG tube from my nose. I didn't realize how far that thing was, stuck in my body, until he yanked it out. As he pulled, I could feel a weird rollercoaster sensation start all the way down in my navel, then travel up to my throat and ultimately end like a tickle out of my nasal cavity. Suddenly, it felt like so much pressure inside of my body was gone, and all I could say was, "Thank god."

My big test came when Dr. N took me to a room and put me in a big machine. A monitor sat nearby, purportedly showing my internal organs. He handed me a viscous, blue liquid in a paper Dixie cup.

"What you're going to do is drink this solution. I know it looks radioactive, but it's fine." He pointed at my abdomen on the screen. "Then we're going to take a look at the monitor and see if any of the solution starts popping out of your esophagus, here, sort of like mini fireworks. If that happens, we might still have a problem, because you'd still be leaking at the connection."

I tensed up. How, after all these days, could it still be possible for there to be a leak in me? I looked at the few ounces of the liquid, my heart racing as I swirled it around the cup. I drank it all in a slow gulp. It tasted like bubble gum.

I looked at the monitor, the bright line of the liquid traveling down my throat, heading to my esophagus and then slowly sliding down the tube in my abdomen. One fluid motion.

"Hey, look at that!" he said. "Good news."

I melted in relief, letting myself think that I was really going to make it out of here alive, that nothing else catastrophic was going to happen. That I was going to be able to see my daughter again, instead of just hearing about her when Jen came down to visit for a few hours every night.

"I think you're ready to start getting solid foods," Dr. N said.

Shortly thereafter, nutritionist showed me how I'd be eating without a stomach. She put out her fist, indicating the size of a meal I could handle now.

"Most of what your stomach does for you is grind food down into a paste so your intestines can pull out the nutrients," she said. "With your esophagus attached straight to your intestines, your body can't do that grinding. You have to do the work in your mouth. You need to chew twice or three times as much before swallowing."

"Okay, that doesn't sound too hard."

The first thing she gave me was a piece of bread.

I took a bite and chewed, the bread melting in my mouth. Then I swallowed and gagged.

"What did that feel like?"

"Eckk. I could feel it hit somewhere in my chest and get stuck. But the feeling went away, I guess."

"That's okay. Your body has to get used to something new. It'll take some time."

And, sure enough, within a week I was eating a slice of pizza, chewing until my jaw ached.

As time went on, more of the monitors started to go away. They took one IV out of my arm and then the other. The little green pain medication button went away, too, replaced by liquid medicine and pills that I had to take four times a day. I started to get anxious for home, to get my life back to some sense of normalcy.

I started being able to take more visitors. One of them, a seventy-five-year-old client of mine named Hank, would bring manila envelopes with dirty jokes and pictures and tell me to hide it under my bed from my wife. He was like a father, friend, client, and mentor all wrapped in one. I couldn't die and let him down.

The moment my head felt clear enough to use my laptop, I started trying to reconnect with some of the people in my life. I emailed old clients and friends, telling them I made it out of the surgery okay. I wanted people to treat me normal again. I felt entirely disconnected from the world outside of this hundred-square-foot hospital room.

A client named Joe called me one day after I had emailed him.

"Steve, you're alive!" he said.

"Barely," I laughed. I was surprised by the comment. I hadn't told him I was going to be in the hospital because I thought I would have been out within a week.

"Yeah, Judy from Stein & Co. called and asked if I had heard about you. She said you were in a coma and told me she wanted to make sure I was 'taken care of' going forward."

"Oh yeah? Didn't know the vultures were circling. Well, Joe, listen, I'm back and I'll be out of the hospital and ready to take care of you in just a few days."

"Okay, Steve. Well, really you should just focus on yourself right now but I appreciate it."

About two weeks after I came out of the coma, once I was finally down to just one wire hanging out of my body—an electrode, measuring my heart rate—I asked Jen to bring Mia down to Stanford. I already felt like I was missing so many little occasions that I'd never see again. She was walking several steps at a time without falling, Jen had told me. And she was almost talking. I thought about her almost constantly.

Mia was hanging over Jen's shoulder facing backwards when she came into the room. Jen turned her to me, and she wriggled in her arms, looking at me curiously. She was so much more expressive than the last time I had seen her. Her cheeks were fuller, her hair growing in. When I saw her face, all this pain, this struggle, seemed worth it. I knew I would make it through any misery to know her and to see her grow and for her to have a father.

Jen offered her to me, and I hugged her into my chest. She wiggled uncomfortably for a second until something clicked and she seemed to remember who I was. Then she giggled and slackened.

I looked into her eyes. "I'm still here. I'm still here."

# CHAPTER

# EIGHT

 As I neared four weeks in the hospital, each day seemed like it would never end. Friends who would previously visit for a few hours now only came for thirty minutes and I had seen the same episodes of *Frasier* at least ten times.

Finally, when I was reduced to just two monitors at my bedside, the doctors told me it was time go home. I was overjoyed, at first, to sleep in my own bed again under a real comforter, without monitors beeping at me to remind me every second: *Hey, shithead, you're still pretty messed up!*

But I also felt nervous, like a kindergartener getting dropped off at school for the first time and realizing that I was duped, that my mom was totally leaving me here by myself. After a month of having people check on me every five minutes, telling me not to worry, that this was all normal, now I had to do it all on my own. I had to be able to tell whether or not a smelly fart was all good, or meant I was dying. It was too much.

My release day was a cloudy Thursday at the end of February. I had clambered into a pair of sweatpants, which felt constricting after I had spent more than a month wearing an ass-less dress. The muscles in my arms and legs had withered, and my skin hung loose with stretch marks. I could still barely stand without feeling lightheaded, and the nurses made me get into a wheelchair to leave the building. Jen put Mia in my lap as I sagged in the chair. My cracked ribs hurt under my hoodie, and I breathed half as much as normal to avoid the pain.

I wrapped both arms around Mia and kissed her forehead. She squirmed in my lap, probably still skeptical whether this man with biceps the size of bananas was her father. I held her in tight, and she eventually settled in. The wisps of blond hair were starting to fill out her head. I thought about all the little hairs that had grown in while I was gone.

I made motor sounds and lightly shook Mia as an attending wheeled us out the front door into the blinding sun. The early-spring air swirling around the Stanford campus was biting.

"Ready to go home?" Jen said.

"I'm ready to go anywhere outside of this hospital."

Jen buckled Mia into her car seat while I struggled into the passenger seat. Our first stop on the way home was the pharmacy, where I picked up such a massive quantity of opioids that the doctor had put a special seal on the prescription, making it look like a letter from the president. It would have made a junkie salivate.

I read the directions to Jen in the car. Up to four doses of OxyContin per day, one Oxycodone in the morning, and a liquid form of Vicodin called Lortab to be used "as needed." I also had a fentanyl patch to place on my arm.

"That seems like a lot," Jen said. "I mean, doesn't that seem like a lot?"

"I guess. But they're doctors. They prescribed it to me for a reason." I opened the Lortab and took my first swig. It felt "needed."

As we drove home, winding our way past the ticky-tacky houses of Daly City on the hour-long trek up the peninsula, the vistas I had gotten so used to over the years took on a new life. Jennifer drove in the right lane on the Golden Gate Bridge, and I rolled down the window to feel the fresh bay wind whipping sideways across the span. The Marin hills popped with California's impossible winter green, reminding me of the amazing nonsense of West Coast seasons. The pain in my abdomen faded, and I closed my eyes and rode the rollercoaster wave in my body as the car zoomed down the hill toward Tiburon.

"It feels like it's been so long since I've seen all of this. I don't think I've looked at it—like, *really* looked at it, in years," I told Jen.

She smiled a little bit and nodded. A tear edged its way out of the corner of her eye. She quickly wiped it away. I looked at her for a few seconds, unsure of what to say, then turned back out the window.

The engine hummed up the Tiburon ridge to our driveway. From my hospital bed, I had been anticipating this moment, what it would feel like when I finally pulled up to my house again. But now, I just felt like I wasn't home. I was just at a house. A huge, extremely shiny house.

A pile of groceries was lined up on the kitchen counter like I was a contestant on *Chopped.* Jen had gone all out: cheeses, yogurts, fat-free yogurts, fruit, soups — everything.

"I wanted to make sure we got a lot of different things for you to try. I also got a recipe book with a lot of low-fat, no-spice things we can try out."

"Thank you. I mean, really, thank you. I'm just not really hungry."

"Oh, okay. Well, I'll go put Mia in her crib. Do you mind if I heat something up for myself? I'm starving."

"Of course."

She looked deflated as she left the room.

It wasn't her fault, but in truth this whole focus on food was frustrating. I had always had a strange and somewhat hostile relationship with food, since the time I was a kid. Because my adoptive parents, the people who took me in and loved me in a way no one else had, were both obese, I had a super-sense attuned to hearing the little snickers behind our backs every time they came to one of my school events. I felt embarrassed that food could hold such a grip over someone, asking myself, *why is it so hard for them to just stop? Just stop eating.*

Probably because of that, I've always looked at food not really as something to be enjoyed in and of itself, but as a means to an end. It was fuel to get me through the day. It was a reason to meet up with friends. It was a sponge so the liquor wouldn't get us drunk as quickly. When I had a nice meal, I enjoyed the taste of course, but in general I never really cared if I was eating at a Michelin-starred restaurant or at a gas station, gorging myself on a burrito.

But now, my whole life was about to revolve around food. Just being in the hospital for a month had brought me down from almost one seventy to about one hundred forty-five pounds. The doctors gave me six weeks until I'd have to start chemotherapy, which was probably going to make me lose more weight. So before I left the hospital Dr. N had encouraged me to try to pack on as much weight as I could, like a bear before winter hibernation.

Feeling bad that I had shut Jen down, I asked her an hour later to make me a smoothie. She jumped at the chance and handed me a purple concoction. I took a sip of it at the kitchen counter and said *nopenopenope* before heading to the sink and vomiting it right back up.

"Aghh, I'm sorry," I said. "It tasted really good, I swear."

"It's okay, we've got a lot more stuff you can try."

"I think I'll wait until the morning, if that's okay."

"Do whatever you need to do," she said. She wrapped her hand around my wrist. "Go get some rest."

The next morning, after taking one immediate-release OxyCodone, a slow-release OxyContin and a swig of the Lortab, I tried Greek yogurt. Unlike the smoothie, I could hold it down, but it seemed to stick in my abdomen like a lump for the next six hours.

Later that day, I found what seemed like the Goldilocks—a mini-bagel with a little bit of cream cheese and some jam on top. It packed a lot of calories in a small package that didn't hurt on the way down. But still, after just one of those I felt like I had gorged myself on a sixteen-ounce filet. After eating it I had to go lie down on the couch for more than an hour before getting back up to think about the next thing that I'd have to put into my body.

I couldn't drink water. Setting aside the fact that it didn't have any calories and took up valuable internal real estate, any amount of it made me double over with nausea. It was as if I had gulped a whole gallon and tried to do a hundred-yard sprint after just a tiny sip. I quickly got used to my throat feeling like sandpaper.

So, to hydrate, I spent about a half-hour every day standing at the kitchen counter with a bottle of Gatorade, pouring it into a shot glass that said *Maui Was Wowee!* Holding the little glass, I imagined I was back at a college party, drinking cheap plastic bottles of vodka, and then tossed back the shot of Arctic Freeze. I'd gag for a few seconds and toss my head onto the counter, standing there and grunting until the burning in my esophagus settled back into a dull nausea. Then repeat.

The pain medication did its own part to both sap any actual appetite I had and make me constipated beyond belief. Each meal was painful to think about, as I'd force food down my throat just to have it sit in my intestines for hours without movement. But I couldn't reduce my dosage of the pills with my ribs still healing underneath the skin.

I knew things in my life would be different after my stomach was removed, but I wasn't imagining it to be the dull, frustrating, all-encompassing level of different that I was now experiencing. I thought it was going to be *big* things that caused me issues, like having my intestines bust while I bleed out on the floor. But the fact that all of these small things that I just couldn't do anymore were piling up was almost worse. At least the other way would have been a quick death.

\* \* \*

Sex, or rather the absence of it, hung over me like a cloud. I completely lost my drive, and Jen didn't seem to have much interest in doing it, or at least in doing it with me. More than the cancer, more than the weight I had shed, more than any incontinence, that basic lack of any sexual intimacy brought me down and made me feel like I just wasn't a man anymore.

To top it all off, at my first chemotherapy consultation, just a few days after I got back home from the hospital, my oncologist told me that there was a strong possibility I'd come out the other side of the chemo infertile. It might last a few years, or it might be for the rest of my life.

On the way home from that appointment, I thought of how to tell Jen. The topic of children was always a fraught one for Jen and me. Since we had gotten married, our plans were to have two kids. But having children on command wasn't as easy as we thought. I could tell it wounded Jen, but she always put on a strong face, and we tried until she carried Mia through until birth. After that, we didn't talk much about the second kid. But I still always assumed we were on the same page in wanting two.

I waited until we got into bed to tell her about the appointment.

"The doctor says I might be infertile when I'm done with chemo."

"Oh. Wow."

"What do you think about that?"

"How can we even *be* thinking about that right now? We are just trying to get through the day. You don't want to have another child now, do you? This doesn't seem like the ideal time."

"No, I agree. But what if we want to have one later? Maybe once chemotherapy is over, we will want to have another baby."

She stayed silent, looking me in the eyes.

"I think I should go to the sperm bank before I start chemo," I said. "Just in case it affects my fertility. Or, I don't know, what if I'm gone and you wanted to have another…"

"Don't talk like that."

"Okay, I'm sorry, I'm just —"

"If you think it's a good idea to go to the sperm bank, go do it. I don't know if I'm ever going to want to go through what we went through again, but if it makes you feel better, do it."

I could see in her eyes that she was afraid. Afraid, probably, of the possibility that we would have another baby and then I would die. But I still had that dream of having two kids, and I wanted to keep thinking about the future.

A week later, I walked into a sperm bank in an office building in the Mission District of San Francisco. The lobby had a fish tank, and a young woman sat behind a glass wall at reception.

"You'll be donating today?" she asked.

"Yes. Well, wait, no. It's for me, or I mean for my wife, for the future. Like if we want to have kids. I'm going through chemotherapy in a few weeks."

"I'm sorry to hear that. So, you'll be using storage?"

"That sounds right."

She had me fill out a form that seemed to be gauging whether or not I was an alpha-male. *What is your IQ? How often do you exercise per week?*

"Do I have to fill all this in if I'm just storing? I mean, this isn't going to go out to *other people,* is it?"

"No, we'll store it in a separate room for you. Just fill in whatever you can." Then she handed me a plastic container. "You'll deposit your specimen in here and then place it in this paper bag. Inside the room you'll find any materials you might need."

"Materials?"

"Yes, *materials.*"

"Oh. Got it."

I walked through two doors into a sterile white room that had a flatscreen TV, a table, and a hilariously out-of-place leather chaise lounge. I sat down and browsed the "materials" on the table. They had everything a vanilla person like me could ever dream of: Mature, Teen, Lesbian, Cancer Patients Gone Wild. Okay, I made one of those up.

I decided to spice up my life and went with Asian Persuasion. Doing the business in this room with two cracked ribs had to have been the least sexual experience in my life, but eventually I did my duty and gave the bag to someone wearing scrubs outside. Then I waited about fifteen minutes before a doctor called me into his office. He looked like he had just rolled out of bed.

"Steve, is it? It's not good news. You don't have anything."

"Don't have any what?"

"Sperm. You've got nothing. Zero."

"What? I did a test a few years ago, and the count was like a hundred eighty million."

"Mm, impressive. But no. You're heading into war with a water gun. Come take a look."

He put a slide under a microscope, and I looked inside. It looked like an acid trip.

"What am I looking for?"

"Do you see anything moving?"

"No."

"Exactly."

"Oh."

"You said you're going through chemotherapy in a few weeks?"

"Yeah. They told me I might become infertile from those drugs. But I didn't think it would've happened already. I still wanted one more kid."

"I'm sorry. It's still possible your system could rebound in the future. But I don't want to get you too hopeful. The chances aren't high."

In the lobby, the receptionist asked me for my insurance information, but I paid cash and went home. I passed Jen in the living room. I didn't say anything about what happened, and she didn't ask. I got in bed, feeling the full weight of yet another part of my life being taken away from me. Mia would grow up an only child, because of me. I couldn't be a father to another child. I wasn't being a husband to Jen. Was I really a man anymore?

Mia started crying over the baby monitor, and I heard Jen call from across the house.

"Steeeve, can you take care of her? I'm in the middle of a call."

Still mad at how cruel life had been to me, I trudged up the stairs to the baby's room. Her toys were lying all over the floor, and I had to dodge around them like landmines to get to the crib. Mia was wailing inside, flailing her arms and legs in every direction. What the hell did she even want? I picked her up, and she looked at me and immediately stopped crying. She reached her tiny hand out and touched my face. Right then, everything else melted away, and I teared up. How could I be so stuck on the fact that I couldn't have another kid? I was worried about the future and couldn't see the present, with her gummy smile, right in front of me. I puffed out my cheeks, and she giggled at me and tossed her head back. Then I set Mia back down in her crib, the wailing replaced with small whines, and watched her until she fell asleep. I already had everything I wanted, right here.

\* \* \*

As the California rain dried up and the windy bayside winter turned into spring, I had not only failed at putting on any weight, but I actually went in the opposite direction and lost ten pounds. Just in time to start chemotherapy.

I had intentionally kept myself oblivious to what chemotherapy actually entailed. I hated the idea of the cancer patient who was defined by their disease and nothing else, talking about their trials and triumphs in every conversation. In my head, if I didn't know everything about chemotherapy, if I just showed up and let it happen, it wouldn't overtake me and become the entirety of my life.

The only things I really knew about chemo were that people got sick and they lost their hair. If I'm honest, I was more worried about the second side effect than the first, fearing that it would be a glaring signal to the whole world of how messed up I was.

My first chemotherapy appointment at the Stanford Cancer Center was on a sunny Monday morning. I thought about asking Jen to drive me, given that the warning label on my medication advised against driving, but she had a meeting with a client.

As I walked inside the medical office, they led me into in a large, warmly lit room that had ten or so reclining La-Z-Boy chairs lining the walls. Piano music was emanating softly from a speaker I couldn't see, and the sound of Wolf Blitzer's voice came at a low volume from a TV.

I sank into one of the recliners and lay back as a nurse gave me an anti-nausea drug called Zofran. On a metal pole to my right, she hung a clear bag about the size of a football filled with liquid. Then she pricked me in my left arm, and the bag started to drip.

"Just sit here and relax," she said softly. This was the kind of place where everyone talked almost in whispers, as if we were all in on a secret together.

I watched the liquid *drip ... drip... drip ...* out of the bag. A chill slowly headed up my forearm, into my shoulder and then nestled into my chest as my body filled with goosebumps. The nurse brought me a heated blanket. Strangely, I felt more comfortable here in this chair than I did almost anywhere in my home. It didn't hurt at all.

Looking around the room, I saw the gamut of cancer patients. One guy, wearing a polo shirt and boat shoes, looked like he was just battling a common cold. A pale woman in the chair next to him, on the other hand, had skin hanging from her neck like she had recently been thirty pounds heavier. She sat silently looking straight ahead the entire time I was there. I wondered which one of the two I would look like after a few weeks doing this.

About thirty minutes in, when half of my bag was empty, a man in a wheelchair was rolled into the room. His cheeks and eyelids sagged like a bloodhound, and his eyes flamed red. He could have been in his sixties or his eighties. A nurse brought him to the chair next to mine and helped him up.

"Thank you, thank you," he said. He settled in and rolled up the right sleeve of his flannel shirt. Ropy veins protruded from his forearm, and the nurse easily found a vein. He leaned back and sighed, then looked over at me. I averted my eyes, embarrassed at having stared at him the whole time.

He smiled, all lips. "Hello. New here?"

"First day," I said, trying to return the smile.

"Happy first day. I'm George."

"Steve."

"You know how I knew it was your first day? You've got that waiting look, like you're wondering what's going to happen, instead of the look everyone else here has. Resigned, or angry."

"You don't seem to have that look."

"I did for a long time."

"Does it always feel so cold in here?"

"The fluid will do that to you. Funny thing to me is that I always feel the cold go down from my top to my bottom, and every time it ends right at my ass. Never fails."

"Oh my god. You're so right!" I laughed. He joined in. "How much longer do you have? I mean, sorry. How long do you have for the chemo?"

He chuckled softly. "That's alright. I'm on my fourth week, so I've got just a couple of days left. Pancreatic. Last time it was my prostate."

"I'm sorry to hear that. I had stomach cancer. Or ... I *have* stomach cancer. I'm not really sure which one to say. I don't have a stomach anymore, so should I be saying I have stomach cancer?"

"Quite the pickle."

"How does it feel after four weeks?"

"Oh, you manage. Haven't had to pay for a haircut in months. I'll take what I can get. I didn't really want to do it this time around, but that didn't fly with the wife. So here I am." He leaned back in his chair and sighed.

"Wow. She's making you do it?"

"Well, no. But I could just see how much it was going to tear her up if I didn't. I'm just doing what I can."

I wondered if Jen would feel the same if I didn't want to do the chemo. Were we going to be like this man and his wife in thirty years? Somehow, it didn't feel like it.

George and I passed the next half-hour chatting idly, as the bags to our sides slowly dripped down.

When the last drop sank into the tube, I was ready to hop out of my recliner, but the nurse came back and plopped a second bag on the pole.

"Another one?" I asked.

George responded instead of the nurse. "You'll be lucky if it's only two."

He was right—after the second one, they grabbed a third bag. The rest of the time I was there, I tuned in and out of the TV as my ass fell asleep.

"I almost wish it was painful," I told George. "Might be better than this."

"Careful what you wish for," he said with a laugh. "It doesn't hit you from the front. It'll sneak around your back with a thousand tiny cuts."

Finally, after more than an hour and a half in that chair, they sent me on my way with a new prescription for chemotherapy drugs. I only had to do the reclining-chair chemo once a week, and the rest of the week I'd have to take pills that were the size of olives five times a day.

As I drove back home, I thought of the tired faces of the other people in those recliners. I wondered how much pain they were in, how much pain I'd soon be in. But, since it didn't really hurt at all, I allowed myself to think for a brief moment that maybe I'd be able to make it out of this okay. That maybe I was somehow *different* from all those other people.

# CHAPTER

# NINE

Two days after my first chemotherapy appointment, I felt a constant chill through my body. I was completely stuffed up, like I had a case of the flu multiplied by ten. I was huddled under a blanket in bed when I got a call from an assistant of a Stanford oncologist saying I needed to come down for a CT scan. I had enough of these done already to know what was going on. They wanted to find out if I still had any cancerous masses, or if I was in remission. We scheduled an appointment for the very next day.

At the doctor's office, they injected me with something called a contrast, which warmed my body up starting from my arm, up to my shoulder and down my abdomen. Then I lay down on a white board outside of a big cylinder of a machine. Supposedly, the contrast was going to light up the inside of my body for the doctors to see.

"When you go inside, take in a deep breath and put your arms in the air," he told me, then left the room. The machine made a *brrrrrrrp* sound as the bed slid into the tube, and in thirty seconds, it was over. A nurse led me into another room, where I sat waiting for my sentence. I started working up my speech to Jen if they found that the cancer had spread.

The doctor walked in the room, straight-faced. *Is that a bad sign?*

"Ok, you're good to go. We'll give you a call in about seven days for your results."

"A week?"

"Yes. It'll take a while to interpret the results, unfortunately."

"So, next Wednesday?"

"Oh no, sorry, seven business days. Friday."

So, the countdown began. For the next week, I was a nervous wreck, dreading that the knowledge of whether I was going to live or die was out there in a test result sitting in an envelope somewhere. I didn't feel like I could talk to Jen about it. She would just say: "Let's wait to get the results until we start worrying." The unknown was pointless, for her.

Instead, I called PJ Gallaway. He coughed when he answered the phone, then seemed to be shushing some kids before he spoke.

"Hello?"

"Hey, PJ. It's Steve, your cancer twin."

"Cancer twin! You kill me. How's it going Steve? I heard from Dr. N your surgery went well. Really glad to hear that."

"Yeah, I think I made it out with a couple more battle scars than you did, unfortunately. But I'm hanging in there."

I told him about the CT scan, unloading all of my fear into the phone like I was talking to my therapist.

"Okay, there's a term for this," he said. "Get a load of this one: scan-xiety. I've had it every time I've gotten a scan. So basically, you're waiting for the most momentous results of your life. It's like taking your final exams and waiting for your grade, except worse. At least in school you knew whether you studied or not, so you could reasonably predict whether you did well. Here, you have no idea until that exact moment of the big reveal."

"Honestly, I couldn't have said it better. What do you do about it?"

"Excuse me for a second." He seemed to cover the mouthpiece and cough, loudly and dryly. "Sorry. Well, I usually try to find something to distract myself. Read a book."

"I haven't read anything longer than a prescription label in three months."

"Ha! Then watch a movie. Or thirty movies. Just know, you can make it through this. Hey, sorry to cut it short, but I've got to go. Wife's calling my name. Hang in there, Steve."

We hung up and I went to bed with a small relief. I could put a name to what I was feeling: Scan-xiety. At least I wasn't the only one in the world feeling this.

Finally, at 9:01 a.m. the next Friday, I called Stanford and asked the sleepy woman on the phone if she had the results.

"Yes, we have your results. When would you like to set up your appointment?"

"My appointment for what?"

"To get your results."

"Can't you just tell me over the phone? It's an hour away."

"I'm sorry, sir, but no. Those are just the rules," she said.

"Okay, then. I'll set up an appointment."

"When would you like to set an appointment for?"

"An hour from now."

"I'm sorry. The earliest we have available is Monday afternoon."

"What!" I cursed into the phone.

"Would you like me to schedule you for Monday?"

"Yes, I'll take the appointment."

Another three days passed. My heart rate was constantly elevated, every sound in the house practically causing me to jump out of my seat. It seemed fishy to me that they wouldn't tell me what my results were. That must mean something bad. People always want to deliver bad news in person. If it was good news, the operator would have been thrilled to be the one to deliver it.

I finally made the drive down to Stanford on Monday afternoon. A young woman with red hair was behind the desk at the oncology department. I wondered if she was the same person who was on the phone.

"Can you tell me the results of my CT scan?" I asked. "My name's Steve Melen."

"I'm sorry, you're going to have to wait for the doctor. Please have a seat."

"Come on, I know you have it! Just open up the chart!"

She silently waved her hand toward the waiting room.

I plopped down grumbling in the chair, wondering why the fuck they couldn't just greet me with a *Congratulations, you're not dying!* Or a *Sorry, bud, maybe next time you'll beat the big C!*

I looked around the room and saw sick people. People so beaten and shrunken to the point of near death, people who couldn't walk, people who looked like they were ready to die after maybe three full rounds of chemotherapy, some who were crying, some who seemed resigned to their fates, some—

"Steve," a nurse called.

Finally! I followed the woman into the hallway. She walked too slowly as she took me to a scale to take my weight. *For the love of fucking god, just give me the results, just give me the results.*

She sat me down in a chair and started to take my blood pressure.

"It's a little high," she said.

"Mm, gotcha." *No shit, give me my goddamn results, and then maybe we can test it.*

She finally led me into the doctor's office.

"Dr. F will see you in a few minutes," she said and shut the door on her way out.

Another ten minutes, and finally there was a sound right outside the door of someone pulling charts from their holder. In walked Dr. F, the red-faced, slightly bloated oncologist who was now assigned to me. He was smiling. Another doctor trailed him into the office.

"How ya doing?" Dr. F asked too enthusiastically as he patted me on the knee.

"How am I doing? How *am* I doing, doc?"

"Well, everything's great! We didn't find anything out of the ordinary in the scans. Other than the fact that you don't have a stomach!" He boomed with laughter.

"Oh my god," I said. I felt an enormous, physical pressure come off my body. I didn't realize my jaw had been clenched. I stretched it and it popped.

He pulled out a copy of the scan from the file.

"You've got a little module here, but it looks like nothing, probably just scar tissue. It's all great!"

Within a second, everything had changed. I wouldn't have to go home and break the news to Jen. Really, there wasn't any news at all. For once in the past half-year, there was *nothing* to talk about. That was the best thing that could have happened to me. My head collapsed into my hands, and I started crying. The other doctor brought me a few tissues and let me have it out.

"It's good news, Steve."

"I know, I know." I sniffled and tried to recompose myself. "So, what's next?"

"Well, we already cut out everything. So next we just need to make sure nothing grows back. That's why we're getting you started on the radiation in a couple weeks. *Zap!*"

"What's radiation going to be like?"

"Oh, well, people's reactions to radiation go all across the spectrum. Some people handle it really well, and others have ... a tougher time. But you're relatively young, so I think you'll do well."

"Okay, thanks. By the way, I'm almost out of some of the pain medication they prescribed to me. Any chance I could get another prescription?"

"Sure, sure," he said absently. "Which ones do you need?"

"What's the delayed release one? Oxy-"

"OxyContin. Sure thing. Just so you know, in some areas of the country people have been getting hooked on OxyContin. I'm not too worried about you, though. You seem like a smart guy." He looked to the other doctor in the room. "Give Mr. Melen here anything he might need to stay comfortable."

Dr. F shook my hand and left the room, reiterating his hopes for me. The other doctor mumbled a warning about side effects and signed a prescription with a wave of his hand.

When I left Stanford, I felt like I had to celebrate. In the past, that would have meant taking a tequila shot and staying up into the small hours of the morning with friends. But after that appointment, after finding out I was going to stay alive for at least a few more months, I went to a gas station, bought a chocolate Whatchamacallit bar, and ate it alone in my car.

* * *

Things didn't get any less lonely from there. Friends weren't visiting me or calling just to chat, but instead to "check up on me." Jen seemed focused on work. She never said it, but I was suspicious that she was working so much because she was still sure I was going to die. She was preparing to support Mia as a single mother.

But I tried to settle into a routine as the days of chemo wore on. When I woke up in the morning, I took my chemotherapy pills and some pain meds to moderate the flu-like symptoms. Then I tried to get some work done, because my firm was still technically employing me for god knows what reason. My boss, ever the willing critic before, praised me every time I lifted a finger. As far as I could tell, they just didn't know what to do with me. I don't think they had ever had a thirty-eight-year-old employee become a cancer patient. But one thing was for sure: they didn't want me coming in the office, so they let me know gently I could work from home as much as I needed.

One day, as I sat in front of my computer, the words switched around with each other on my emails while my mind tried to defog. A tanker's horn sounded outside on the bay, and I looked at the morning marine layer slowly peeling back outside my window. The sun peeked out, the first time after several straight days of rain. I thought about the years before my surgery, when Jen and I would walk down from the hills to a trail along the bay and a beautiful stretch of greenery on the shoreline called Blackie's Pasture. This was before the baby, when our conversations were always positive and hopeful, and we would talk about our happy memories together. Those were the times when, even if I still had my uncertainty about our marriage, I felt like we could really build something together. Like if we put our minds to it and committed ourselves, we could continue to create a loving family.

Watching the bay water sparkle in the sun from my couch, I felt the urge to get outside and try to walk, to reclaim a piece of that optimistic past life. I hadn't gone more than the distance from my bedroom to the kitchen in weeks.

Instead of walking down the hill, I resigned myself to driving to Blackie's Pasture for a short walk along the bay. I put on a pair of sweats and an oversized hoodie that would reveal nothing about how much weight I had lost, then draped a baseball cap low over my forehead like a celebrity in public.

As I got in the car, though, I felt a wave of anxiety. What are my neighbors going to think of me when they see my ghost-white skin, my sunken cheeks? Will they think I'm a junkie?

I prepared a defense in my head: *No need to be alarmed, Janet. I'm not a heroin addict. I'm just a cancer patient. How long do I have to live? Let me check my watch.*

I parked in the lot and got out of the car. The wind was strong as the fog floated over the bay. I put my foot up on the back bumper to stretch. My insides hurt as my body got used to moving in ways it hadn't since the surgery.

An elderly woman in a puffy jacket was closing her trunk next to me. She held her gaze on my face for just a second longer than normal. I gave her a sort of awkward half wave, then felt embarrassed and retracted my hand. She flashed a small smile back at me, then started walking away.

"I bet you've never met a person without a stomach, have you?" I blurted in her direction. I didn't know why I said it. Some part of me must have just needed human interaction, and I didn't know what else to say.

She stopped and pulled her head back in slight surprise, as if to say, *Who, me?*

"What do you mean?" she asked.

"I'm sorry, I just noticed you looking at me."

"Oh, I didn't mean t—"

"No, no it's okay. I know I look like crap right now. Believe me, when I look in the mirror, I can't believe it. But if you think I look bad now, you should've seen me a month ago. I had cancer and got my stomach removed."

She seemed at a loss for words for a moment, and we stared quietly at each other. "I—I didn't know you could keep going without a stomach. Are you able to eat?"

I told her about the past two months of my life, and she listened intently. I never went on my walk, because she and I spent the next half hour talking at my car. She told me about her husband passing away the previous year. We shared brief stories together, sitting on our respective bumpers, and then I left to drive back home.

I had driven down to the park ashamed of my story, but I realized on the drive home that my story was emblazoned on my face and body, whether I liked it or not. I realized in that moment that the only way I'd be able to get back to normal life was through radical honesty. Maybe other people would be like her, and they'd use that honesty to get some things off their own chest.

* * *

Once I got to the second week of chemo, nausea became a constant. I started each day dry heaving over the toilet until my muscles ached. Then I'd lie in bed for hours, curled in a ball, rocking my body and moaning to release pent-up energy. Jen tried to help me as much as she could, making me soups and anything else she thought I could eat, but I felt guilty that she had to take on this role. I tried to ask for as little help as possible. I took two extra doses of Lortab every day, but it just sent me into an endless cycle that dulled the pain but kept me nauseated while making it almost impossible to eat a substantive meal.

Finally, I heard through the grapevine that there might be a golden ticket to address all my issues at once: marijuana. I googled doctors who specialize in medicinal marijuana and found one in San Francisco. That same day I went to his office, which was on the second floor of a record shop.

A large landscape painting was the only thing filling the reception area. At the far end, a young woman with a number of facial piercings was texting behind the receptionist's desk. Two kids with skateboards were sitting in the waiting room filling out forms. As I approached the desk, the woman perked up. I must have been the sickest person she had seen in a while.

After I filled out the forms, the doctor, who looked like a combination of the two men in the Big Lebowski, called my name. He led me to an office that looked like it belonged to a businessman who just got canned. There was nothing, literally nothing, inside except for an executive desk, a rolling chair for him and a folding chair for me.

"So, tell me how you're feeling," he said, pulling out a blank sheet of computer paper and clicking a pen.

"Well, I'm recovering from cancer..."

"That must be horrible." He scribbled on the paper.

"Um, yeah. Anyway, I heard that marijuana could be helpful for my nausea and maybe give me an appetite."

"Medicinal cannabis is known to have a number of benefits among all patients. Tell me something: What made you smile today?"

"What made me smile?"

"Yes. Has anything made you smile? I find it's helpful to think of the small positives when we are in a dark time."

"I mean, it's only 11 a.m. But, seeing my daughter, I guess?"

He nodded once ... twice ... three times, his eyes closed. Then he scribbled more on the piece of computer paper. I could hear the ticking of a clock somewhere, but the walls were bare.

"Remember that everything you need is within you." He reached into the desk and pulled out a pad, then signed a small sheet of paper. "Bring this to Mandy at the front desk, and she'll give you your forms."

"Uh, okay. Thanks."

"Thank you, friend."

At the front desk, Mandy momentarily looked up from her phone to take the signed slip of paper. Then she gave me another form, and within five minutes I was out the door and headed to an office in San Rafael to get my medical marijuana card.

I went straight to the dispensary down the street from there. The employees seemed to take their roles much more seriously than the doctor, as they informed me of the varying strains, strengths, tastes and feelings of their arsenal.

I felt intimidated but excited, like a kid on his first trip to Disney World. "The most I ever smoked was in college, and I'd just smoke whatever someone else had. But today's a new day. Sell me."

I left with a pipe, an ounce of some purple kush, some ointments, and some Rice Krispie treats, and even a couple of seedling plants so I could try to grow my own. Why the hell not?

Back home, I tried smoking the kush. But after one hit from the pipe I dissolved into a minutes-long coughing spell that made my swollen ribs ache. I gave up on smoking and ate a Rice Krispie treat instead.

Several minutes in, I didn't feel high, and I wondered if maybe they had given me a regular snack. The treat had tasted nothing like the skunky, disgusting "special" confections we made back in college.

But about an hour in, I suddenly got extremely hungry. I ate a lunchbox-sized cup of plain yogurt, and it went down smoothly. It almost felt like I had a stomach again. Soon after, the tightness I had felt in my abdomen lightened, and my focus re-centered on my head. It was a beautiful feeling. Whereas before, getting a heady high might have made me anxious or paranoid, now it was the only thing that had taken my mind off the pain in months.

I sat on my deck and looked out to the San Francisco Bay. A sailboat passed by slowly down the crystal blue strait between Angel Island and Tiburon, and one lone paddleboarder waded slowly through the water. I felt completely relaxed, present to the moment. I wasn't worried about anything that was coming.

Jen was at work, and Fabiana was in the kitchen cooking something while Mia napped. I went into Mia's room and picked her up. She slowly stirred from her nap, stretching her arms and legs out as she blinked her eyes open. Then she started crying. But that was okay, because even if she was crying, I was still here, holding her. I held her and brought her downstairs into bed with me. When Jen got home from work later that evening, she smiled when she came in the bedroom. She got in bed on the other side of Mia.

That night, everything was okay. We were a family.

# CHAPTER
## TEN

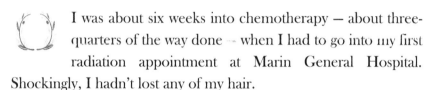 I was about six weeks into chemotherapy — about three-quarters of the way done — when I had to go into my first radiation appointment at Marin General Hospital. Shockingly, I hadn't lost any of my hair.

Dr. P, a radiation oncologist, told me they were going to set me up with eight weeks of radiation, Monday through Friday, with the weekends off.

"It won't feel too bad at first, but it's going to build up. You're going to lose a lot of your energy."

"Lose it? I spend twenty hours a day in bed. Not sure how much worse I can get."

He led me into an office with a huge machine shaped like a giant blender. I assumed it would be frapping up my insides. I took my shirt off and crossed my arms, trying to hide the ribs protruding from my body. The surgery scars across my left side stood at attention like a coat hanger brand.

The doctor took an ink gun and gave me three tiny tattoos dotting the area from my ribcage to my navel along my left side. Over the next several years, I'd learn these tattoos are a hallmark of cancer patients gone through radiation—everybody has them. Insiders all show them to each other, like the numbers that

Auschwitz victims bear on their arms. A constant reminder of tough times.

"I've always been too chicken to get a tattoo," I told the doctor.

"Well, if you're going to get one, you can't get one much less noticeable than this."

"Maybe this will be my inspiration to get a giant dragon across my back."

Finally, the big machine in the corner of the room whirred to life. A device at the end of the machine slowly lined up a metallic mouth that interlocked like a zipper on my three tattoos.

"While that's on you, don't move," he said. "You don't want it to zap somewhere it's not meant to."

The touch of the metal was cold on my skin. I closed my eyes and took a deep breath, then held it for ten seconds. The machine made a long beeping sound below me.

"Ok, you can move."

I hadn't felt anything. "That was it?"

"Three more times, and then that's it," he said.

Within ten minutes flat, I was out the door. I felt nothing when I left, even more nothing when I went to bed that night.

But if chemotherapy is like getting slowly poisoned, radiation is like having someone pull out your internal organs while you're asleep, punch them and then put them back inside your body.

After the fourth day of my treatments, I woke up with a thick wad of phlegm in the back of my throat. Jennifer was already out of bed, probably doing work in the office upstairs. I wanted to call to her, to ask if she could make me a cup of tea, but I didn't want to interrupt her. I could hear Fabiana rustling somewhere in the house, cooing things in Spanish to the baby. Everyone else was doing things with their lives, and I was down here thinking how hard it would be to get out of bed.

I slowly stood up to spit in the bathroom. The room narrowed into a tunnel, and glowing ants started crawling across my vision. I sat back down on the edge of the bed and took a breath, and the ants started to fade.

I sat there for a while, unable to convince myself to get back up again. But when the feeling in the bottom of my throat turned from a tickle into a burn, I ran in a hunch, stood over the toilet, and hacked. The spit came out gray with little pulpy chunks inside it.

"What the hell could that be?" I asked out loud. I hadn't eaten anything in more than a day. *Is that — me? Is that part of my body? Am I shedding like a snake?* The thought almost brought me to puking again.

Over the next several days, I could basically only get out of bed to go to my radiation appointments. My body ached more and more, and eating anything—even the Rice Krispie treats—hurt my entire abdomen. One night, I woke up with searing pain in my waist. It felt like my intestines were literally moving inside me, and my body was making the noises to match. Jen shot up in bed and frantically asked if I needed to go to the ER. I said no. I just wanted it to stop, to not need her and everyone else to be caring for me all the time.

While the chemotherapy mostly made me feel nauseous and ill, the radiation seemed to cause actual, physical pain everywhere around those three tattoos. Two OxyContins taken one after another numbed it, but they also left my mind in such a fog that I couldn't do much of anything besides watch TV. The constant through it all was that girl from the Progressive car insurance commercials, Flo. I saw her more than any other human being in that period. Sometimes, I imagined intricate scenes where we went on a blind date together. Other times, I just imagined strangling her.

One evening, I was lying in bed flipping between the same four channels I had been watching over the past few weeks. I reached toward the nightstand, over the cup that contained my flesh-filled phlegm and to the water cup. I sat up in bed and took a tiny sip, tossing my head back to give the water a clear path past my esophagus and straight down into my intestines. It didn't work—it felt like acid corroding down the inside of my neck. I dashed to the bathroom to vomit, and more chunks came out.

I kept the medicine cabinet permanently open to avoid looking at myself, which meant instead that I looked at the label of my Oxycontin bottle. I popped one and swallowed it without water, hoping that the extended release would just put me to sleep already and take me out of my misery.

But it didn't work, so I decided I'd try to go upstairs and sleep in my reclining chair. Grabbing onto the handrail of the staircase to support me, I stutter-stepped up, pulling my body one step at a time. When I got to the top, I realized that I had forgotten my blanket downstairs.

*Oh, my god, I've got to go back down,* I thought, and I crumpled onto the floor and cried.

I called Jennifer's name, and she came out from her office and rubbed my back.

"What's wrong? Are you hurt?" she asked.

Sobbing, I asked her to go get me the blanket from downstairs. She looked at me with pity, then walked downstairs and was back up in just a second.

"God, I'd kill to be you," I said.

"It's okay. You're going to be okay."

She helped me over to the recliner in the living room and watched TV with me for a little while as I tried to breathe deeply to settle my body. She rocked Mia in her lap and kept looking over at me as beads of sweat started to go down my face.

Suddenly, my intestines felt like they had twisted in on themselves again, and I yelled out.

Jen stood up and hovered over me. "Steve. I think we need to go to the emergency room."

I tried to keep breathing. "No, no, I think it'll pass." But it hit again, and every muscle in my body felt like it had tightened at once.

"Aggggggh!"

"Come on, we've got to go. I can't stand here and watch you like this."

She pulled me up out of the chair and put me in the car, then strapped Mia into the car seat. She sped to the ER, and the doctors took me immediately. Another bout of pain hit as a nurse helped me to the bed, and I crumpled onto the floor screaming. The doctors came over and gave me a shot of Dilaudid, and then another one as I kept screaming. I vomited into a pail on the floor, while someone told me I needed to get up and into bed.

"You think I can get up right now?"

The doctors made me check in for the night and hooked me up to an IV bag. Eventually, more out of exhaustion than out of any relief, I fell asleep.

Soon after I woke up the next morning, a nurse came in my room with a stretcher.

"Oh god, what now?"

"I'm here to take you to your radiation appointment."

"Right now? Can't I have a sick day?"

"It's best not to."

"Okay. Well, I think I can walk to it. I'm feeling better actually."

"We have to take you on the stretcher. It's hospital procedure."

"You're going to take me to my radiation appointment on a stretcher."

"We're going to take you to an ambulance, which will take you to your radiation appointment."

"Wait, I'm at Marin General right?"

"Yes."

"My radiation appointment is next door to the hospital."

"It's across the street."

"Wait, wait. I have to ride in an ambulance to go a hundred feet? Just let my wife take me over there! I don't want to pay for that."

"Yes, I'm sorry, sir. It's for your own safety."

Her look made it abundantly clear that that was the final say on the matter. So, I hopped in the ambulance for a ten-second ride to the front door of the radiation center.

"So, are you going to mail me my bill?" I asked the paramedic.

"Yeah, actually let me get your mailing address."

After the radiation appointment, they released me from the ER. They told me that what I had experienced was called intussusception, which happens when your intestines literally fold over on top of each other, causing excruciating pain. It was hard to do anything about it, so they just gave me the same directions everyone else had given me: Rest.

When I got back home, my nausea had settled a little bit, and I had more energy. Once again, I allowed myself to think that the worst was over, that I could only recover from here. But that only lasted a day before the symptoms escalated even further, with more vomiting, constipation, and nausea.

I couldn't get out of bed anymore. I had to listen to Mia upstairs, playing, laughing and crying, and I agonized over the distance between where I was now and being the father I wanted to be.

Besides that, I worried about possibly having to go back to the hospital, about all the bills we'd be paying, about ever seeing the other side of the radiation treatments. Was I dragging our family down? Was I just a burden now? At my last few chemotherapy appointments, I was now one of the people who looked worst off in the room. I was angry at the *drip, drip, drip* of the chemo bags, wondering while I shivered with cold why the fuck they hadn't invented a way to just put it all inside my body all at once. A cop pulled me over for speeding on the way back home from one of those appointments, but when he saw my face he let me go without even a warning.

Everything felt so dark. When I texted my friends or P.J., everyone told me to look for the light at the end of the tunnel. But the only light I saw was the dull blue of the TV screen playing the same movies over and over again. I took pain pills just to knock myself out for a few hours at a time. I couldn't even think about the next day. It was hour by hour. I felt ready to just let the cancer come back and kill me. It felt like I was coming to my end. I'm not a religious person, and I had no idea where I'd be going if I died. I thought of my first experience with death: when my adoptive mother died so suddenly, so unexpectedly.

\* \* \*

It happened in November 1990, two years after I started college. I was on a sorority's boat cruise and ended up staying the night with a girl I liked. I woke up late in the morning with a momentary freak-out after forgetting someone else had slept in my bed. When I went downstairs, my roommate was already in the kitchen.

"Your dad called last night. He asked for you to call him back."

"Did he say what it was?"

He shrugged.

I called his number, and he picked up after one ring.

"Steve, what are you doing right now?"

"Nothing. I'm just at home. What's up?"

"Your mom had a heart attack last night."

My mind went blank.

"Wh-what?" I paused. "Where is she?" This was the only way I could think of asking what I really meant but couldn't say—is she alive?

"She's at the hospital." His voice was shaking. It felt unfamiliar. He told me the story, and I half-listened, already far away.

Apparently, my dad and mom were going to meet at Vallco Shopping Mall to get dinner at Benihana. They came from work and took separate cars, but on the way home, my mom started having sharp chest pains. She made it all the way to the parking lot and then collapsed outside of her car. I had never heard my dad cry before, but he sobbed the whole time he told the story.

I got on the next flight to San Jose and met my dad in the waiting room. He hugged me hard, tears in his eyes, and told me he loved me. I was jolted—he never said that.

A couple of our extended family members and my grandma surrounded my mom's bed. There was a small TV impossibly high on the wall, and a big window that made the space too bright for the scene inside. She was lying with her head back, with a breathing tube extending from her mouth.

I walked to her bed and took her hand. She was conscious. Her eyes were wide with fear, her hand limp in mine.

Her mouth quivered. She was struggling to say something, but she couldn't muster more than opening and closing her mouth a little. Then she slowly took her hand out of mine and extended her finger. She drew an outline on my wrist: I-C-E.

"You want ice?" I asked.

She nodded.

I felt stupid and hurt that her message was a request for ice and not to say she loved me, but I chastised myself. Who knows what I would have wanted if I was in a hospital bed? I got her some ice chips and helped her eat, then sat with her for several hours. After a while, she fell asleep and my grandmother and I decided to go home and get a few hours of rest.

I lay awake in bed all that night until my door clucked with a gentle knock. My grandma walked into my room and sat on my bed.

Don't say it. *Don't fucking say it.*

"Steve, your mom passed away this morning."

A numb feeling wrapped itself around me like a cold blanket. For a moment, I felt nothing. I was hollow.

I went through the motions after that. We went to the hospital, and the doctors showed us her body. I felt like I barely saw her, like my eyes had cataracts, but the image of my dead mother apparently seared itself into my consciousness on a deeper level, and it would haunt me for years after.

When the funeral came around, several hundred people showed up, including more than a hundred kids she had taught at her school in East San Jose. I had always been somewhat ashamed of my mother and her weight, but in that moment, I felt so proud. I just wished I could have told her. She was only 52.

Now, as I lay in my own bed, suspended in a state somewhere between death and life, I felt grateful for the way she went. When you die suddenly, everyone can remember you exactly as you always were. But when it happens slowly, people have time to acclimate themselves to this new you. To the one who looks feeble and sick and tired and angry, and who might snap at you without warning or burst into tears when you walk in the room.

*I can't live like this,* I thought. *I can't put my family through this pain.*

I took out my laptop and went to Google. Then I typed in the words that I never had the guts to type before.

*Five year survival rate, stage IIIB stomach cancer.*

I clicked on the first link and scrolled down to a graph. Eighty-five percent survival rate. No, wait: eighty-five percent *mortality* rate.

I stared at that chart for a long time. What the hell was I doing, wasting my time with all of this chemotherapy and radiation, making myself even sicker when the odds were already so stacked against me? Why was I living my life in pain, going to appointments that were just making my inevitable death more miserable. I didn't want to spend my short life doing this. I *wouldn't* spend my life living like this.

* * *

The next Monday was my seventh week in radiation. When I heard for the hundredth time, that irradiated *zap* which spewed invisible death into my body, I was just done. The *unfairness* of it all, that I had to go through more pain than anyone else I knew, for what? A *fifteen* percent chance I'd survive? What the hell was the point? I was weeping inside of the machine.

Dr. P stopped the machine and stepped into the room. "Steve, you okay in here? We've got just a few more minutes."

"No ... No, I'm not! I want to do this for my family, for my friends, for all the people who expect me to, but I just can't do it. I can't, I can't."

I waited for him to give me the pump-up speech, to tell me that I just had to power through. I already prepared my response: he didn't know what I was going through, if he was feeling this, he'd say the same thing.

He looked at me for a long time, his glasses sitting low on his nose as his knuckles folded in and out of his hands. "Today is your last day," he said.

"What?"

"You did ninety percent of your radiation. That's honestly more than I thought you'd do. We can call it there."

"What? Are you kidding?"

He smiled. "No. You did great, Steve. I'm really proud of you for sticking it out this far."

I couldn't believe it worked. Finally, some good news. Christ. It was over. "Oh, thank you. Thank you so much."

"Congratulations, you made it through. We can give you a new prescription to help you get through the next few weeks while your body recovers."

"Thank you."

I walked out, and everything I had felt in bed that night seemed a little more distant. I gave a weak smile to the woman at the front desk. She handed me a certificate, signed by all the hospital staff. *You've successfully completed your treatment at Marin County Radiation Center!* Hand-drawn hearts were all over it. I lingered at one person's short note, *Good luck!* Then I remembered: *Fifteen percent.* Even after a small victory, I was reminded that luck was the only thing that would get me through this.

I leaned the certificate on the mantle at home, hoping that someday, if I stared at it enough times, I would feel some sense of accomplishment about what I had been through.

# CHAPTER
## ELEVEN

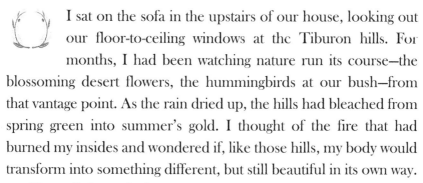I sat on the sofa in the upstairs of our house, looking out our floor-to-ceiling windows at the Tiburon hills. For months, I had been watching nature run its course—the blossoming desert flowers, the hummingbirds at our bush—from that vantage point. As the rain dried up, the hills had bleached from spring green into summer's gold. I thought of the fire that had burned my insides and wondered if, like those hills, my body would transform into something different, but still beautiful in its own way.

Up until the end of radiation, I had a clear path: just survive the surgery, then get through two months of chemotherapy, and finally those weeks of radiation. But with it all over, I now just sat in a sort of limbo, unsure of what I should do next, as my sickness became the worst thing I could imagine: a routine.

Fabiana, the nanny, now rang the doorbell at 7 a.m. every day, two hours earlier than in the past. That was because of a particularly painful agreement Jen and I made after I went through a days-long puking spell that reverberated throughout the house.

"It's just, you never know what a kid is going to remember or carry with them, right?" Jen had said. "Like, is she going to have memories of you being really sick?"

"Yeah, maybe she'll have a complex and only be able to date men who have a colostomy bag."

"No, but really. I'm serious, what do you think?"

"Maybe it's better to just let her see the truth."

She shrugged, seeming like she wasn't going to push it any further.

"I'm mostly kidding," I said. "I think you're probably right, as shitty as it is to admit."

We decided that Mia's exposure to me should be limited during the morning, when I was at my worst before the pain medication kicked in. So each day Fabiana came in, made a quick breakfast for Mia and then took her out of the house—to the park, to the movies, wherever—while I started the long process of dealing with the day's pain.

At this point, in addition to the fentanyl patch on my shoulder and the "as needed" liquid Vicodin, of which I drank so much that it started to taste like dessert, I was taking one immediate-release Oxycodone in the morning and three or four slow-release OxyContins throughout the day, along with Reglan for nausea, Ativan for anxiety and marijuana for my appetite.

The pills made it hard to do much else besides watch cable. I frequently couldn't even pay attention to a two-hour long movie, so when I did watch movies, I stuck with ones heavy on action and thin on plot (although I did manage to catch The Shawshank Redemption approximately fifty million times).

Around 3 p.m., I braced myself to skip a pill to have a clear head for when Mia and Fabiana returned. I could always get in about an hour of playtime. It was my favorite part of the day, and I approached it with the zeal that I used to carry to my work. One day, before they got back, I gathered up a bag of Mia's toys and brought them down into the master bedroom, scattering them all over the floor. I pulled clean clothes out of the dryer and stuck them in a pile on the bed. Rushing upstairs when the door opened, I took Mia and brought her to the bedroom. Knowing what was coming, she stuck her arms out like an airplane. I wound her up in my arms—oooone, twooooo, THREE!—and threw her onto the pile of clothes. A muffled giggle wafted from the pile. Immediately after, I had to lie down, wincing from the pain in my ribcage, while she played with her toys on the ground. Still, I felt overjoyed that I could still bring my baby girl some happiness.

She had already gotten her legs underneath her and was just starting to talk. She was in the phase where her only possible form of self-transportation was to *run, run, run.*

"Mia, play with this over here!" I said, holding out a noisy sand-filled ball. She looked up at me, those baby teeth filling her mouth like pieces of white bubblegum, and a big smile went across her face.

Then I hid the toy behind my back, only to produce it and roll it to her at the end of the bed. She tried to get up onto the bed but failed to hook her foot and fell. I slowly moved over to her and guiltily used all of my strength to pull her onto the bed.

"Ready?"

She slapped her hands down and nodded furiously.

I threw the pile of clothes up into the air, and she spread her arms wide as socks and underwear floated down like confetti and covered her.

I lay there laughing as much as I ever have, even as I knew my body would hate me later.

When I felt like I couldn't keep my eyes open any longer, I called Fabiana. She came downstairs and took Mia to her room. Like a construction worker coming home after a long day of physical labor, I fell into an exhausted but satisfied sleep.

* * * * *

On a sunny Tuesday, Rider, who had been my anesthesiologist during the second surgery, invited me to lunch at one of those outdoor spots in an interchangeable downtown drag in Silicon Valley. He wanted to catch up and see how I was doing, six months after I had had my surgery.

Rider came dressed smartly in a pair of chinos and a dress shirt. He looked every part of a successful doctor. Meanwhile, I screamed unemployment in my pullover hoodie and loose sweatpants, while my pale, sunken face shouted illness. As soon as I walked in, I noticed a pair of men a few tables over start to stare as if I had leprosy.

"You have no idea how good it is to see you," Rider said when we sat down. "I had never seen anything like it. I mean, I deal with a lot in the hospital. But it's so much harder when it's someone I know, when it was you."

I nodded. I couldn't take my attention off the two men at the adjacent table, now obviously staring at me. The younger guy, after taking a sip of his drink, would cock his head just so I was in his periphery, then look back and talk to the other one in a lower voice. I imagined their conversation: *What's the matter with him? That dude looks like a corpse.*

"I really thought we were going to lose you for a while there."

"What? Oh, yeah. Well here I am!"

"Anyway, I'm just really glad to see you."

When the server came around, Rider ordered a beer.

"Same," I said.

Rider looked at me sideways.

"Sorry, I should have ordered a coke. You really shouldn't be drinking. Maybe a glass of champagne on New Year's or your birthday, but in general..."

"Come on, man! You ordered one. Let me live a little."

He put his hands up. "Alright! You win! Just try not to make it a habit."

The beers arrived, and I took a tiny sip. I immediately felt like I had to burp.

"Hey, did you ever write that letter to your daughter?" he asked.

I punched my chest and held it in. "Did I write my death letter? Do I look like the type who's going to go gracefully into death? There was no freaking way."

"Well, regardless, I think it's still a good idea to do it," he said. Then he seemed to catch himself. "I mean, I think I should do it myself for my kids, too, you know, just in case."

"I just feel like I'd be giving up if I did that. I need to spend every second *fighting* for her."

"I mean, they aren't mutually exclusive."

We took a look at the menu. He got a burger, and I got a side salad, knowing I'd probably only be able to get two bites down.

My watch triple-beeped at me, the first of three alarms I had set for the day. "Time to take my warm and fuzzy pill," I said as I reached into my bag and grabbed my OxyContin bottle. I popped one into my mouth and swallowed it with a sip of the water.

He was silent for a few seconds. "What pills do they have you taking right now?"

"Oh, you know, a purple one, a round one, another one that's the size of a cashew. There's this one that they told me is called Viagra."

"Really, though." He wasn't in a jokey mood. No one was particularly jokey with me lately, and it was starting to bother me.

I told him the contents of my home pharmacy. He slowly raised his eyebrows as the list continued. Then he sat back and sighed.

"Jesus." He paused for a long time. "Listen, I don't want to be preachy here, but that's going to get you at some point."

"Going to get me?"

"Yeah. The pill thing. It's gonna catch up to you."

I got defensive as I realized what he was implying. "I'm not an addict. I'm not some junkie buying heroin off the street. I'm in pain, and my doctors are prescribing these to me."

"Hey, hey, I get it. I really do. I don't blame you at all. You've just got to understand—that stuff used to be end-of-life drugs. This was what you would get for battlefield injuries. If you don't want to end your life, and I hope you don't, you're going to have to confront it. It's not if—it's when."

"Okay, I appreciate the concern, but what am I supposed to do? I'm literally just one foot in front of the other right now."

"Fine. Just one piece of advice, and I'll leave it. Don't go shopping for scrips. Have just one doctor who can control you, who can wean you off of the drugs as you heal. You've been through enough. Don't make it harder on yourself."

"Fine. Noted."

After our meal, Rider picked up the tab, and I looked down at my plate and felt accomplished—I had gotten down three bites.

I thought about what Rider had said the whole way home. Up to that point, I had trusted everything the doctors had said and prescribed as being in my best interest. Was Rider telling me I shouldn't trust them? I was still feeling this pain. Every second, every day.

But still, the next morning as I popped open bottle after bottle, his voice was in the back of my head. I was suddenly hyper-aware of the fact that I was taking *four* different pain medications, some of them four times a day. *The pill thing is going to get you,* his voice told me as I struggled to remember whether it had been five hours since I had taken the OxyContin or if I was confusing it with the Lortab. It was all a blur of a dosages, of forty-milligrams, twenty-milligrams, two-ounces twice-per-day, three-times-per-day.

So I had an idea to appease Rider's stupid voice in my head: If I could reduce myself to just taking one type of pill, I could better understand what was going into my body. Then, I'd be able to monitor what I was taking. I decided to only take the OxyContin, since those pills were control-released and could last for several hours at a time.

First, I took the fentanyl patch off my arm with little problem. Then, I got rid of the Lortab, literally pouring it all down the sink like I was in a movie and the cops were about to bust me.

That one stung a little more, as I could feel a semi-constant throbbing near my esophagus and an ache in my ribs that made it hard to move my torso. I upped my daily dosage of OxyContin by one pill a day.

The next elimination target was the immediate-release Oxycodone, which I had been taking in the morning to kick-start my day. The first day I skipped the Oxycodone, though, I lay trapped in my bed until noon, so I kept one of those in my routine every morning.

But even still, I felt better about what I was doing. I even told Jen about it while we were brushing our teeth one night.

"I really feel like, now that I'm down to just one type of med, I'll be able to see what I'm doing and come off it."

"I'm proud of you. How long do you think it will take?"

"Well, I don't know. I guess I'll just feel it out?"

\* \* \* \*

A week later, while Jennifer was out of town, I was reaching for a cup in the top cabinet of the kitchen when my vision started to blur. The kitchen became a tunnel. I started to fall, but I caught myself on the counter just before hitting the corner of the marble.

I stood there supporting myself. I felt ashamed, imagining Fabiana coming home with Mia to find me passed out, bleeding onto the floor from the head. Frightened, I set up an appointment to see my oncologist.

Dr. F's normally big smile evaporated the moment he looked at me in his Stanford office. *Do I look even worse than I thought?*

"Steve—how are you feeling?" he said, trying to sound casual.

"Everything's rosy," I said.

"You look like you've lost weight."

"Really? I thought I had put on a few pounds."

He laughed abruptly, then beckoned me outside of the office to a scale. It was one of those mechanical contraptions that had a weight and a seesaw on both sides.

"You still use one of these? Here, at Stanford?"

"Sometimes we got things right the first time we made them. Step up, please."

The weight was set on one hundred thirty pounds. If I had stepped on it a year earlier, the right side would have flown down with a *clunk*. This time, though, the scale didn't budge, and Dr. F traced his pointer finger along the dial. One twenty-five, one twenty, one fifteen—

"Christ," I said, as he finally stopped where the sides held evenly. He clicked his pen and wrote the number down in ink on his chart.

*One hundred pounds.* I weighed a hundred and seventy-five right before the surgery in January. Eight months later, I, a man more than six feet tall, now weighed as much as a twelve-year-old. My breath shortened, and I grabbed onto the scale for support. I wanted to cry.

"You okay, Steve?"

"I just don't know what to do. I've been doing everything you guys have told me. How can I keep going? My two-year-old daughter's going to weigh more than me soon."

He laughed and put his hand on my shoulder. "I think you've still got a few years to worry about that," he said. "Your body is a lot different now, Steve. You don't have a stomach as a holding tank for all your food, so it's hard to keep your weight."

But he said he didn't want me to lose any *more* weight, so he signed me up for something called Total Parenteral Nutrition, or TPN. A doctor would stick an IV in my arm that went directly into one of my main arteries, he explained. For several hours a day, I'd have to carry a backpack that had fluids going straight into my bloodstream.

"Jesus, I'm going to look like a kid going to school!" I said. But I was in no position to say no, so I relented.

Two days later, I had a tube hanging out of my left bicep and a few dozen vials of life-force in my fridge. Each morning, after my first two pills, I'd carefully sanitize the nozzle at the end of my arm—necessary because there was a high risk of an infection that could go straight to my heart—and hooked up the fluids.

Wearing the backpack, I tried to get on with my day as normally as possible. But getting the TPN had a huge psychological effect on me. Before, I knew that I felt sick and that, to a certain extent, I looked sick. But now, every time I looked at the clear, round nozzle hanging out of my arm, I was reminded that my body wasn't able to keep itself alive, that it needed something external to get the job done. If I had been born a hundred years earlier—hell, maybe even twenty years earlier—I would have been dead already.

The TPN did help me level off my weight loss, but it made me retreat further into myself. As I spent hours each day sanitizing, monitoring and just carrying the fluids around with me, now it really felt like my life revolved around my sickness. There was just no way to get around it. Jennifer barely seemed to look at me while we talked anymore. The only times we really got to chat were at dinner, when Jen cooked a meal for herself, then steamed some vegetables for the baby and for me. All we talked about in those moments was either Mia's day or my day. Never the future. Never *our* future.

The only crystal ball I had during that time, the only guiding light, was P.J. Gallaway. Often, when I would start thinking about the big picture, about that fifteen-percent survival rate now so prominently etched into my skull, I'd call P.J. just to hear his voice, to know that if he was okay, at least I'd be alive three months from now. He'd listen to me talk about how scared I was, tell me I should talk to my wife more, and end with the advice, "If I can make it, I know you can." He had a tendency, though, to descend into coughing fits while we were on the phone, so sometimes he couldn't get it out.

"Are you okay?" I'd ask, silently freaking out.

"Oh, I'm fine, I'm fine," he'd say. "Just a cold I get when the seasons change."

Well, the seasons are kind of *always* changing, right? So, hard to refute him on that.

My friendships started to fall into two categories: the people who stopped reaching out, probably because they thought I was going to die and there likely seemed no point, and the friends who did reach out but quietly treated every conversation like it would be our last. They often seemed like drunk drivers attempting to pass a field sobriety test, working desperately to get everything perfectly correct but stumbling because of how hard they were trying.

Buddy, my best friend from college who was at my bedside when I started coding in the hospital, fell into the second category. One day, when he was set to come over for wine on my back porch, I took an extra OxyContin. I wanted to have a good time, and I didn't want to be in pain. I brought out a bottle of wine and two glasses.

"Can you drink now?" he asked.

"This is my second drink since the surgery. But I've got to live a little, you know?"

He normally had a big laugh, but now it was small, short, like an uncertain teenager. "How has work been going?"

"These days it's mostly just about stopping the bleeding. A lot of: 'No, no, I'm good. I can still take care of you and handle your money.' 'You sure?' 'Definitely!'"

He sat quiet for a minute. I could see his mind working, looking like he was trying to defuse an intricate bomb just in having this conversation with me. *Cut the blue cable, for the love of god, don't touch the red one!*

I broke the silence. "You saw Scott got married?"

He lit up. "Yes! I never thought he was going to find someone who would make him settle down."

"Crazy."

We sat looking out on the hillside, drinking our wine. I got buzzed after just half a glass: a by-product of not having a stomach anymore, I figured.

"What's that in your arm?" Buddy asked, pointing at the nozzle for the TPN.

"Oh, god. It's nothing." I didn't want to talk about my illness, about all the loose skin hanging off my body. I knew that the easiest way to get a few get well cards in the mail but never actually see anyone was to have people pity me. But still, the conversation always managed to end up back on my illness.

He took a sip of wine, and we sat in an uncomfortable silence.

I remembered the woman in the back of her car down at Blackie's Pasture. *Wear your story.*

"I mean, actually, it's pretty crazy," I said. "This thing's called a PICC line. It literally goes up a vein in my arm and into an artery straight into my heart! You could probably blow into it like a balloon and put me into cardiac arrest."

Finally, Buddy's real laugh was back. "I'll remember that for the next time you piss me off, Melen."

It was like we had let some of the air out of an overstuffed balloon. After that, we could just sit there and talk, just like before. I felt completely content. We finished our glasses and then poured another. Before I had time to really get buzzed, I was drunk.

"Those pain pills make me feel sooooo goood," I said. I put sunglasses on, even though the sun had already set. "OxyContin. For real. Feels like I could fly off the deck."

Buddy laughed. "Careful there. Don't want you to fly straight into the bay."

"Oh, you know, I'll be okay. As long as you're here." I wrapped an arm around him.

"Alright, bud —"

"Hey, that's your name."

"Yep ... yep. Let's get you to sleep, maybe."

"Okey dokey, then."

We went inside and said our goodbyes, and he said goodnight to Jen from the doorway. He seemed in a rush to get out of there. I went into the living room, where Jen was sitting watching a movie. I sat down and looked at her.

"Heeeey Jen. Question: Do you ever want to have some sex with me?"

"What? Are you okay?"

"Yeah yeah. I'm feeling good. Buddy and I had some wine outside."

"Oh."

"Soooooo?"

"Can we talk about this later?"

I shook my head. "Mm-mm."

"It's just, it's just really hard to think about that right now. With everything that's going on."

"Am I being a good huzzband?"

"You're doing everything you can right now, Steve. I'm really proud of you. Why don't you go get some sleep?"

"Okay. Okaaaaaaaaay. See you tomorrow morning."

"Goodnight, Steve."

# CHAPTER
# TWELVE

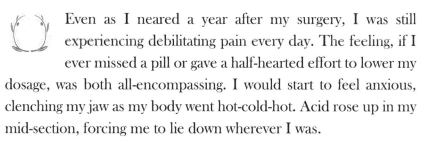 Even as I neared a year after my surgery, I was still experiencing debilitating pain every day. The feeling, if I ever missed a pill or gave a half-hearted effort to lower my dosage, was both all-encompassing. I would start to feel anxious, clenching my jaw as my body went hot-cold-hot. Acid rose up in my mid-section, forcing me to lie down wherever I was.

If that was all, maybe I would have told myself that I had a problem. But that wasn't it: the pain was also incredibly specific. I swore that I could feel my esophagus throbbing under my chest. The scar where the doctors cut me open seemed to pulsate, and my left ribs still ached.

It felt like the pain medication was the only thing keeping my body from rejecting this new, strange form it had taken.

In September, I had been taking five OxyContins a day, every three hours, in addition to the morning Oxycodone. But then the pain started to rise every two and a half hours, so I added an extra pill. And then it came every two hours.

I heard Rider's voice in my head: *They're going to get you at some point.* I offered my response to his imaginary nagging: *You don't feel the pain I'm going through.*

One morning when I popped an Oxy from the medicine cabinet, Jen quietly said: "You've been taking a few more of those."

*They're going to get you.*

I snapped back: "I already quit the other pills. The doctors are prescribing me this, so this is what they want me to take. I still need it."

She silently left the bathroom.

More than ever before, Jen and I were running in parallel orbits, circling each other without ever really colliding. She occupied her space to finish her work, while I laid claim to all of the dark areas in the house lit by TVs. There were days at a time in which I didn't feel like I saw her, or if I did, we barely said more than a few sentences to each other.

At a certain point, an invisible, unspoken-of wall went up between us. We were living such different lives, like friends from high school who came back home from college to find they've got nothing in common anymore. She had to go to sleep every night next to a man who smelled like death, who woke up every two hours to puke. Like everyone else, I think she had long ago determined I was going to die, and she was preparing herself mentally and financially for living as a widow with a two-year-old daughter. And I had to go to sleep next to *what-should-have-been* — the person who was slowly working her way to attaining everything I wanted. Our relationship had been founded on partying, fun, and excitement, and this new reality didn't seem like part of the bargain for either of us.

As the months wore on, my frustrations grew. After days subsiding only on Pedialyte, and feeling the common opiate side effect of being both starving and not hungry at all, one afternoon I bought a pack of See's Candy milk chocolate balls, hoping to stuff a bunch of calories into my body through a small package.

A few hours later, I was back in the hospital, my intestines blocked up like a multi-car wreck on the highway, and I had to get six enemas (six!) in one night to unplug the drain.

"Jesus fucking Christ, it was just a piece of chocolate!" I said as I rolled over onto my side for the fifth invasion.

For weeks at a time, my internal drain got so clogged up that I had to resort to doing things that I wouldn't have believed a year earlier. Once, sitting on the toilet after five laxatives and six days without a bowel movement, I yelled and finally, in frustration, stuck my finger up my butt. I could literally *feel* it up there, stuck like an eighteen-wheeler under a too-short bridge. I circled my finger around it until it softened, and when I removed my finger, I finally had my first bowel movement in a week. I sat on the toilet, horrified at myself. Horrified that it actually worked. That I might have to do it again. If someone else had told me about it, I would have found the idea hilarious, but I was too disgusted in myself to find any humor in the situation.

* * *

At the beginning of December, I had entered a kind of stasis. I hadn't gained much weight, but I'd stopped losing it. I was able to muster enough energy for a few phone calls a day, just enough to maintain my current clients at Stein & Co. I could still see Mia for a few hours during the day, even though now I mostly just watched her play from my bed. I thought I was in control of my pill use and felt strangely proud that I could still function while taking the now-seven or eight Oxys per day. Or so I thought.

One evening, I was sitting in the living room watching TV when Jennifer walked in the front door carrying her gym bag. Normally, she'd head downstairs for a shower, but this time she lingered at the entrance to the room.

"Hey." She came around from behind the couch and kissed me on the forehead, then hung over me for a few seconds.

"What's up?"

"I ran into Buddy's sister while doing squats at the club today," she said.

"Oh, yeah? I haven't seen her in forever. How was she doing?"

"She was good," she said. Jen looked great when she came back from the gym, her hair up in a high ponytail, glistening remnants of sweat on her forehead. It made me want to have some semblance of a libido again.

She walked around the couch to the opposite side from my head. I pulled my blanket-covered legs back to give her a spot to sit.

"She said something ... interesting," Jen said.

"Oh. What's that?"

She shifted her legs underneath her and sighed.

"She said that I need to leave you because you have a drug problem."

I was shell-shocked. This was completely out of the blue. *What the hell?* "What? Are you serious? Because I have a drug problem?"

Jennifer nodded.

I started talking louder than I intended to. "I haven't even seen her in five years. How the hell would she know whether or not I have a drug problem?"

I had only seen Buddy once in the past few months, when we had wine on my patio. *Had I been bad enough that he would tell his sister?* I felt a creeping paranoia, one that told me, *She knows because everyone knows because it's the talk of the town because you can't keep yourself fucking together.* I kept the thought to myself.

"I guess maybe she's talked to Buddy?" Jen said.

"Well, what do you think about what she said? Do you think I'm an addict?"

"I—I don't know. I was kind of taken back to hear it. I didn't really say anything."

My paranoia started to turn to anger. I knew what this was—an ultimatum. She wanted to confront me about this, but she didn't want to do it directly. She had to put the blame on someone else's shoulders. *It's not me saying this, look, people are talking about it!*

"You're talking to me like I'm some kind of dopehead. I'm not some guy going out on the street to try to drown out my sorrows about life. I've felt this pain every day, and it's because I had Stage-Three cancer and lost three of my organs. I'm *still feeling it.* Every day. It's still there."

"Steve—"

"You really don't understand, and you can't come at me with this, 'Oh, someone in town said I should do this because...'"

She put her hand up to her face and looked down. I could see tears in her eyes. "I just can't sit here and watch you keep killing yourself!" She started sobbing.

I was about to say something else, but I stopped myself. In that moment, I realized that I had been thinking only of how my actions would help me from one second to the next. I wasn't thinking about how they could affect the people around me. I wasn't seeing this woman in front of me as my wife. Right now, she was something in the way of me getting the prescription I needed next month. "Jen, I, I'm not —"

"How many have you been taking?" she blurted out, for the first time, looking almost surprised that she said it.

"How many pills?"

She nodded.

"I'm just taking what the doctor tells me."

"Stop using that as an excuse. How many?"

"I, I don't know. Seven or eight a day, and one of the other ones in the morning."

"So, you're taking, what, three hundred a month? How can that be normal?"

That number hit me like a brick. Three hundred. I hadn't ever added it up like that. I wouldn't have even been able to fathom that a year ago, and yet here I was. Maybe I *was* an addict.

We were silent for a long time, meeting each other's eyes several times and then unlocking to stare down at the couch.

She broke it: "I know you're going through a lot. But it's just hard to see you do this to yourself."

"You know what, you're probably right. I've been taking too many of these damn things. I'm going to stop. I'll do it."

She breathed out heavily, then smiled weakly and came across the couch. She leaned on my stomach and hugged me. I wanted to ask her to get off, because she was hurting me, but I didn't. Eventually, she got up and went to make me a smoothie.

\* \* \*

A few days later, I went to my primary care doctor to start a plan for weaning myself off the OxyContin. A not-insignificant part of me still believed that my defenses were right—that I had this insolvable pain, and it wasn't the pills that were the issue. But, for the first time in a long while, I allowed for a small possibility that I was wrong. At worst, I'd be able to say, *Aha! I really am as sick as I said. It wasn't just the pills, assholes.*

The doctor applauded me for my effort—*so one doctor gives me as many pills as I want and another wants me to get off them?* — but said I should wean myself slowly. So, I started off January with a prescription for two hundred sixty pills.

I often had to go to multiple pharmacies to pick up my full month's prescription. This time, I phoned in 60 pills to a

Walgreen's in the Castro district of San Francisco and the other two hundred at a CVS across the street. The Castro always had a steady supply of opiates because of the number of AIDS patients who still lived there.

At CVS, the pharmacist asked me several questions, scrutinizing me carefully. But I uttered my version of the magical incantation *open sesame* — "Cancer" — and the walls magically came down. I got my full prescription.

When I got into my car, I double-checked the prescription and the bottle. Prescribed quantity of 200 pills, 20 mg apiece. On the bottle: Quantity 200, 40 mg.

I did a double-take, re-reading the prescription and the bottle, then bottle and prescription. Forty milligrams? Holy shit.

Despite myself, I felt like I had just won the lottery, and I pumped my body up and down in my seat. *Holy shit, holy shit.* Somehow, I had nearly doubled my prescription, just because the pharmacist made a mistake. But wait; I wasn't supposed to feel good about this. I was supposed to be ready to throw this all down the drain, to go back into the pharmacy and say: "Excuse me, I think you gave me the wrong prescription..."

*No,* why would I do that when I wasn't even sure if weaning off the pills would help? I could just take half of each pill at a time, and then stash the other half away in case of emergency.

I didn't want to feel excited, but something deep inside of me did. Maybe it was that same instinct that causes people to gamble away their mortgages at the casino. *Jackpot.*

When I got home, I put one hundred of the pills in an old bottle and stashed it in a shoebox in the top of the closet. I switched the other hundred pills to the 20 mg bottle and threw away the 40 mg bottle.

I went day by day trying to follow the doctor's regimen and reduce myself by a pill a day. But as I went on, I started to get confused. Had I taken a full twenty and a half of a forty that day, or had I mixed them up and just taken half of a twenty? Given the pain I felt, it must have been the latter. Better take an extra twenty to be safe.

Then, the half-pills, being half as big as the regular ones, started to feel like they weren't really the full dosage at all, so I'd pop an extra one in when I felt like I needed it. *It's okay, it's just this one time.*

Jen seemed happier, more animated when she talked about our relationship and our future. We started talking about pre-schools for Mia, about taking trips to Lake Tahoe. Christmas passed by, Mia seeming overjoyed by the plethora of presents placed around the house, and in February I finally hit a year post-surgery.

Jen and I made dinner for that anniversary: a salad with a little bit of vinegar on top, some lentil soup and a cupcake for dessert.

"I'm really proud of how far you've come," she told me.

\* \* \*

Each month, my doctor lowered my prescription by 30 pills. But I kept relying more and more on the stash, eventually needing four of the lower-dosage pills just to get out of bed in the morning. Every time I took the shoebox down from the top of the closet, I thought of how I was letting Jen, Mia, everyone, down. But that shame didn't make the pain go away.

By April, the doctor prescribed me two hundred pills. That was fine, I thought, I would just have to cut back on the pills I had been taking out of my emergency stash. Still, a voice in the back of my head told me: *You know you've been taking more than that. The pills are going to get you at some point.* I kept going hour by hour, taking whatever I needed to get out of pain.

It hit me that I was in trouble two weeks into April, when I looked in my regular pill bottle and saw only one layer of tablets lining the bottom. Five pills left, meant to last me two weeks.

I looked in my stash of forty mg tablets, although I already knew what I'd find in the contraband bottle—nothing.

*This has to be a mistake,* I thought.

It wasn't. I had taken two hundred Oxys in two weeks.

I tried to calm myself down. Some cosmic force would intervene to save me, I knew. All I had to do was call my doctor and say the C-word, and then I'd get what I needed and then I could just take a few more pills and I'd be okay.

The operator at my primary care doctor's office told me the doctor was on vacation. I asked if there was anyone else in the office I could speak to. It was an emergency.

"Hold, please," she said, and I rehearsed my speech in my head while I waited.

"Hello, this is Dr. Harris," said a woman's voice.

"Hi, this is Steve Melen. I usually see Dr. Y in your office. He prescribed me some pain pills for cancer recovery last month, but I've been having flare-ups, and I ran out early. I was hoping that you would be able to give me an early refill for the month."

I could hear her typing away in the background, and there was a pause for several seconds.

"No, we're not going to refill you."

*What?* "You—You don't understand—I had my stomach removed, I had Stage IIIb cancer."

"Yes, I do understand. We just prescribed you two weeks ago. You're not due for a new prescription until May. I'm sorry, there's nothing we can do."

I cursed and hung up the phone. I had been getting whatever I wanted, whenever, up until that point, and now I was just cut off, like that.

Panicked, I started wracking my brain for options, and eventually found myself Googling *how to get OxyContin* and on the third page of results found an online pharmacy in Canada that said they could ship to the U.S.

I added one hundred 40-mg pills to my cart online and entered my card information, but I shut my laptop, realizing how crazy this was. *I could go to prison.*

My body started to feel tight, even though I had just taken a pill, and I started to sweat. I tried breathing in deeply and slowly, like my therapist had told me, but breaths were coming in shallow. This was different from a regular panic attack. Jennifer was out of the state. I was alone — *alone.*

Except—

I picked up the phone and went to my contacts, scrolling down to the letter P. Then I did something that I had only done a few times in the past few decades. I called my biological mother.

I heard a soft fizzle in the background of the phone, like something was on the stove. "Hello?"

Hearing her voice brought up a deep feeling within me that made me shake. All those years I never knew her, and now I had a way she could make it up to me. "Hey, Penny, it's Steve." I was trying to keep my voice steady.

"Steve?" she asked, taking a second as if to remember which Steve was calling her. "Steve! My god, it's been so long! How are you doing? How's your baby?"

"She's really, really amazing. She's got these beautiful, blue eyes. And blonde hair."

"Just like her dad once did." A pause. "And how are you?"

"I'm doing okay. Well ... yeah, I'm okay."

I waited for a second to see if she'd respond. The line just fizzled with whatever she was sautéing. "Good, good. Happy late birthday, by the way. I meant to send something."

"That's okay. I was hoping to ask you something, actually. I know you had back surgery last year, and I was wondering if you had any of the pain pills left. My doctor gave me the wrong prescription this month, and now he's out of town, so I can't get the right refill."

A painful silence. I was self-conscious, wondering if she would start the rumor mill too, telling everyone I had a problem. But no, I thought, she wouldn't do that.

"Well, of course, Steve, if you think you need them."

"I do." I started to choke up. "I really do. I just don't know how I can keep going without them."

"Okay, it's going to be okay. Just let me go check my medicine cabinet."

I held the phone away from my face, tears heading down my cheeks. *What am I doing?* This was the first time I had called her in months.

"Steve — I have Hydrocodone in here. Does that work? Will that be okay? I don't know if it's what you're looking for, but it's what I have."

I could hear the desperation in her voice. I could tell that she would do anything, literally *anything* for me at this point to make up for my childhood. How could I take advantage of her like this?

"Actually, never mind—I'm sorry I asked. Thanks, anyway."

"Are you sure? Sorry if it isn't the right stuff, I haven't gotten a prescription in a while."

"No, no, it's not your fault. I'll be okay—really. Thanks, I love you. I'll call soon."

"Okay, I love you."

After hanging up, I sat by the phone for a long time, the tightness in my body replaced by a numb feeling.

*This is it—right now. I have to stop.*

I collapsed to the floor and held my knees in my arms for more than an hour, crying alone in my kitchen.

That night, I reached out to PJ Gallaway to see if he had any advice on getting off pain pills.

"I luckily weaned myself off of those early," he said. "Those things are the devil incarnate. I wish you luck, and I know you can do it."

I didn't have my cancer twin to fall back on for advice. I decided to call Jen, who was in New York, and tell her everything: the emergency stash, running out of the pills, everything.

She was silent for a long time before responding. "Well, thank you for telling me. I can't say I didn't have my suspicions."

"Why didn't you say anything?"

"I had already told you what I wanted, everything else was up to you."

I held in my annoyance. "I'm scared to do this. I just don't know if I'll be able to get through the day without them. I'm still in so much pain."

"Steve. The only way you're going to get out of pain is if you *get off these pills.*"

"I don't know."

Jen rebooked her flight to come home a few days early, then set herself up in the guest bedroom as I prepared to detox. I bought a patch that would slow my heart rate before using my last four pills.

That night, the pain and the panic steadily built to an excruciating crescendo. My insides began to burn. I crawled into bed, and the sheets underneath me turned into a puddle of sweat.

"I need a fucking pill," I said out loud.

Forty-eight hours later, I wished I had a gun beside my bed. I was ready to end it all. It was as if I had the flu and food poisoning at the same time, cranked up to eleven. My ribs felt broken all over again. I was hyper-aware of everything in my body, and my esophagus seemed it was rejecting the new connection to my intestine, deciding, *This isn't natural.*

Jen was in and out of the room, watching this pathetic man writhing on the floor, spewing out spit and snot, moaning and yelling. Fabiana took Mia out of the house two extra hours.

I couldn't take it anymore, and I begged Jen to take me to the ER.

She was skeptical at first. "I think we should wait a couple of hours. You should come down from it soon."

"I'm dying, I'm fucking dying right in front of you," I moaned. "This isn't just detoxing."

"Jesus, okay. Fine." She helped me into the car.

The receptionist at the ER recognized me. "Welcome back," she said as I moaned in pain. A nurse brought out a wheelchair and took me to the back immediately. The doctors were never really sure what to do with me, but that was especially the case this time around. They gave me saline through a tube and ran a full battery of tests, leaving Jennifer and I in the room for thirty minutes. She was holding my hand.

A middle-aged nurse with short hair that curled at the end walked in.

"Your tests looked normal, but in your condition, we can't be too careful. What are you feeling?"

"Like ... I swallowed hot coals." Every muscle pulled itself tight, then loosened against my will. I groaned.

"He's been taking so many every day," Jen told the nurse quietly. "The pills. That must be what it is, right?"

"The symptoms look like it. But with someone who has had the surgeries he has, it's hard to say there isn't something else going on, too."

Jen replied: "But it's been a whole year since the surgery. This can't still be from that. There's no way."

I wanted to tell her that she didn't know what she was talking about, that the pain was *real.* It was in my ribs where they had been cracked, that it was in my chest where my esophagus now connected straight into my small intestine. It was there, and there, and it was *everywhere.*

"Make it fucking stop!" I cried.

"He has to sweat it out," Jen said.

"Nonono, I'm not just going to fucking *sweat* this out. I'm goddamn dying."

"Where does it hurt?" the nurse asked.

I caught a deep breath. "My chest. My stomach, I mean my—Jesus! Everywhere! Just please, help me."

She exchanged glances with Jen. "Do you think you need something to ease the pain for now?" she asked.

"Yes, for the love of—"

"No, you can't give that to him!" Jen interrupted. "That's why we're here in the first place. He can't control it."

The nurse looked at her, then at me, indicating that the final word was mine.

"Jen, I have to."

"Steve, no," she said. "You can't do this. If you take that, I don't ... I don't know how much longer I can do this."

Her face was hard. This was an ultimatum.

We held each other's eyes for a long time, longer than we had in months. Tears were welling up just in the back of hers. She already knew my decision.

"Yes, give it to me," I said. I reached for Jen's hand, asking her to be my partner in this, just for this one last time, but she crossed her arms. "Jen, it's okay. We're in a hospital. They know what they're doing."

She put her head in her hands, sobbing. "I don't know how I can help you. You're on your own now," she said, and left.

The nurse looked at me one last time. I gazed down, ashamed that she was going to make me say it again. "Do it."

She stuck the needle into my IV, and a rush of numbing cold swept up my bicep and into my abdomen, rolling like a wave up to my head and down my legs. My toes tingled.

"Ohhhh my god, oh my god, ohmygod, that feels so much better."

I sat there and breathed deeply for several seconds. After some time the nurse asked me if I wanted another shot, and I giddily said yes.

An hour later, as if I were a completely different person from the writhing mess who came into the ER, I stood up and walked out of the hospital. Jen wouldn't come back to pick me up; she sent her stepfather instead. I was hungry, and we stopped and got a burrito on the way back. I ate almost the whole thing in one sitting.

"You really wolfed that down," he said.

"Yeah. I don't know how I had it in me."

But I did know. Life was so much easier now than it had been just an hour ago because Jen was right. They were all right. I was an addict—full stop. The pills had infected me, making me believe I couldn't live without them, that I was still in pain and *needed* them to keep living.

I wasn't in denial anymore. I knew I had a problem, and I needed to fix it. There was just no getting around it anymore. I had tried to pretend all this time that it wasn't my fault that things weren't going well. Everyone else was just wrong, and they would never know what I was going through. But really, it was my refusal to step back and take stock of what I was doing and how I was affecting the people around me that brought me here.

Before I left the hospital, the doctors had given me a prescription for ten Percocet—a rope to guide me down the cliff before I jumped cold turkey.

Detoxing lasted an entire month—the first week spent mostly on the floor, the second in bed, the third between the couch and the bed, and the fourth mostly upright on the couch.

It was extremely difficult, but once I knew the pain would really be gone once I finished withdrawals, I could see it through to the end. In that sense, it wasn't the hardest thing in the world to quit the opiates.

I no longer thought about whether I looked weak or vulnerable. Now, my thought was: I am weak. I am vulnerable. Where do I go from here?

# PART TWO

PART TWO

# CHAPTER
# THIRTEEN

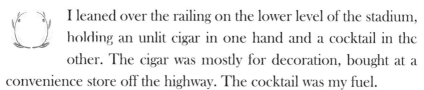 I leaned over the railing on the lower level of the stadium, holding an unlit cigar in one hand and a cocktail in the other. The cigar was mostly for decoration, bought at a convenience store off the highway. The cocktail was my fuel.

It was 2011, two years after the darkest period of my life, and things were completely different. I was now the owner of a racehorse, racing for $400,000 in the highest-stakes competition I had ever been involved with.

Despite the sun's glare against the concrete, a chill was in the air. I had dressed for a Los Angeles winter—tan suit—and the cold running up my arms heightened my nerves. The Hollywood Starlet was our chance to put Killer Graces on the map among the country's best racehorses. She became a 14-1 underdog as the bets poured in. Jerry, the hall-of-famer trainer who assured me our filly would win despite the odds, patted me on the back.

"You know you can watch from up there?" he said, pointing to the closed-off VIP lounge high above the track.

"I like to stay down here, close to the action."

"Suit yourself."

The lower levels were filled with degenerates of every sort: the track regulars carrying fistfuls of betting tickets, the drunk college kids looking for something to do on the weekend, the circles of men discussing who-knows-what in hushed voices. In the bleachers they sang songs, talked too loudly, and swayed after too many beers. Above them, behind the glass walls of the VIP lounge, old boys sat over steak dinners in suits and ties, looking over all the action below and betting in denominations of hundreds instead of singles. Personally, I wanted to be a member of the lounge, but I wanted to hang out in the bleachers.

The buzz grew as the warm-up races gave way to the main event. The herd of two-year-old fillies trotted out onto the track — a show for the betters penciling in last-minute observations. I searched the track for number four and found her at the far end, the tan filly with the jockey in purple. Killer Graces, the horse on which rested so much of my identity now. My comeback horse.

Standing against the railing in my tan suit sized just a little too big to fill out my permanently thin shoulders, I couldn't help but smile. Whether we won the pot or not, I was finally living. Two years after I quit taking opiates, I really had achieved the success that had for so long been derailed.

\* \* \*

Horse racing had become a part of my life before I even got cancer, when I by chance met world-renowned horse owner Paul Luchesi on a flight from Chicago to San Francisco in 2006. Paul was heading to Berkeley to watch one of his best horses, Cause to Believe, race at Golden Gate Fields. If they won the race, they'd be heading to the Kentucky Derby.

We talked at the baggage after we landed, Paul invited me to the race. I said why the hell not, and I went as one of his personal guests. I had seen horses before, but never as close as I did that day, and I was astounded by the size of the thoroughbred Paul owned.

Cause to Believe dominated the race. Afterward, under the gaze of the stadium cameras, Paul strolled out of a ground-level door marked *PERSONNEL ONLY*, beaming a smile in a smart tan suit as he approached his trainer and jockey. "We're heading to the Kentucky Derby!" I heard him say as he excitedly shook hands with each. I stood against the banister and watched as they had their photo taken. Several other faceless trainers waited their turn to shake his hand, beaming like they wanted to ask for his autograph.

I realized then that I wanted exactly what he had: I wanted to be the most exciting person in the room. To be the one who everyone waited in line to shake hands with.

Over the next couple of years, I continued to casually follow Paul's horses, biding my time until I could buy my own. I even attended the Kentucky Derby as Paul's guest, a wild weekend that culminated when I paid a police officer a hundred dollars to shepherd a friend and I, cocktails in hand, sirens blazing, past the horrendous pre-derby traffic straight to the races.

As with everything else in my life, though, the cancer nipped that budding passion, putting a haze of *why bother* over all the things that I used to enjoy. That sentiment continued as I spent my days just thinking about surviving in the year that disappeared into an OxyContin haze.

But after those few long, agonizing weeks of opiate withdrawals in 2009, I faced a novel feeling: I had survived, seemingly in spite of every obstacle that could be thrown my way. I finally could eat a relatively healthy, stable diet without puking and made it back up to 130 pounds. I passed my two-year cancer test (although the doctors only ever said I was in *remission,* an ominous term that only conjured thoughts of the moment the cancer would come back*).* I was almost back to normal, though I had no idea how long that normal would last.

I carried a bucket-list energy with me that came from the knowledge I had made it further than I ever should have but still had a low chance of surviving five more years.

I became excited to do things with Mia again, offering for us to try a new activity every weekend. She got on a bike at age four and ice skates soon after. Jen and I, meanwhile, seemed to come to a silent agreement that even though our relationship would never be the same after I broke her trust in the hospital, perhaps we could raise Mia like a husband-wife business partnership. We were mostly content to keep the status quo, maintaining a functioning family dynamic for Mia's sake.

I craved excitement, freedom, and willed into existence the wildest things that I never dreamt of before. On a whim, I asked Jen and Mia if they would come with me to Minnesota to meet my biological father for the first time.

I had only talked to Ron Miilamenen, Sr., one other time in my life, on the phone, in my early 30s, for a five-minute conversation that was so awkward I was almost expecting him to ask me how my car was running. But this time, I told myself, things would be different. I was a changed man. We set up a meeting in Duluth, Minnesota, at a strange indoor water park that was also a hotel. Ron, who bore a long mustache and a beer belly, was a closed book when we met, greeting me with the impartial, "Hello, Steven." But as we sat down and started to talk, I could see tears come to his eyes, and we spent thirty minutes together talking and crying before hugging and going out to the water park to join the rest of the family.

That was it—the whole trip lasted approximately eight hours, but I was stunned and giddy that I could make something like that happen. *If I can make this happen, what else can I do?*

Well, I thought to myself, I could finally grab that once-budding passion I had by the reins. By 2011, I had started getting in touch with all my old contacts in horse racing, trying to find the right horse to buy. I wanted to feel like I had *made it* again. I wanted to be the guy who struts out of a door marked *PRIVATE* straight onto the racetrack to pat my horse on the head and shake my jockey's hand.

That summer, I got an offer to become a part owner of Killer Graces, a chestnut filly with long, sinewy legs that was trained by hall-of-famer Jerry Dorfer. I leapt at the chance. For our first race—the Cinderella Stakes in Los Angeles—I invited almost everyone I knew by text message, phone call and Facebook invite. The only person who responded was an old high school flame named Tanya, who lived in Southern California and who I hadn't seen in twenty years. I had lost my virginity to Tanya, but I wasn't about to tell Jen about that. I was excited for Tanya and her fiancé, also named Steve and who just happened to be a billionaire, to come to the track, for me to show someone how much of a big-shot I had become.

I still wasn't naturally as energetic as I ever was before I got cancer, so I drank a few vodka sodas at the race, finding it helped me be more social and confident as I tried to fill the shoes of *horse owner.*

We won the race easily, and people at the track patted my back and called me a good luck charm. Tanya and her fiancé were clearly impressed. I felt big.

"You've taken on some new hobbies since we last hung out," Tanya said.

I shrugged, trying to act nonchalant but reveling in the attention. "The trainer does all the work. I just put the money in."

"Well, you know how to pick 'em."

I asked the group if they wanted shots at the bar.

"You can drink alcohol after what happened to you?" Tanya asked.

"Oh, yeah. I just can't drink a lot of liquid, so I like to pack in a lot in a small amount. Hence, *shots!*"

\* \* \*

That was just a few weeks before the Hollywood Starlet, where I sat on the lower levels twiddling my cigar, waiting for the main event. This time, I was solo, just with the trainer and my newer horse mentor, Steve. Yes, Steve's are everywhere but this one was a very successful horse owner, businessman and real estate investor. We would continue our friendship to this day. Jen had to stay back for work. That was okay with me; the racetrack was a place that existed in parallel with the rest of my life. I liked to keep it separate, to have it as an escape.

Killer Graces and the other horses geared up for their race at the far end of the track. Next to me, Steve and also an ancient man with a Native American braid and cowboy boots was nursing a cigarette and talking with a leather-skinned guy wearing mom jeans and white sneakers. They were keeping their voices low, sharing about god knows what sort of conspiracy. The racetrack was a petri dish for the highest, lowest and everyone in between people out there. I loved it.

An announcement came over the intercom, and the jockeys slowly guided their beasts—so much larger in person than on a TV screen—to the starting gates at the far curve of the oval track. Killer Graces lined up in the third gate, with Joe T on top. I sipped the vodka soda in my hand, then winced. I hadn't eaten anything. This was going to get me drunk.

Everything became silent for what felt like an eternity as the jockeys tightened their grips on the reins behind the gates. The drunken ladies in the stands quieted, enraptured. The men high above put their forks and knives down. And here, against the iron railing, it felt like meditation, the final moment of anticipation before it all breaks.

The starting gate opened and was immediately followed by a thousand thunderclaps on the ground. The fillies careened out, their eyes wide with fury. Killer Graces, leaning toward the innermost railing of the track, quickly fell behind to fourth place. They rounded the bend. The jockeys bent perilously forward, working for that one push to take the lead. I leaned over the railing and anxiously sipped my drink.

They curved to the far side of the track, and the sound of the hoofbeats dissipated. I closed my eyes and reveled in the momentary rush of adrenaline. In that moment, I didn't care if Killer Graces won. *This* feeling, right here, was what I was here for.

That feeling evaporated when I remembered how much money was on the line. The other spectators around me silently seemed to agree, clutching their betting tickets and eyeing the scoreboard. The horses worked their way to the second bend. Killer Graces was holding steady in fourth, more than three lengths behind the leader. Not insurmountable, but she'd have to give it every ounce she had to pull ahead.

"Come on, come on," I said.

The trail of dust moved to the beginning of the second bend as the horses started to come back toward us. They flew down the racetrack, kicking up black hell. Suddenly, Killer Graces scampered into third place, then second. I held my breath.

The leather-skinned man grasped a ticket and leaned over the railing. "Hyeeep," he shouted. Now I could hear the sounds of individual hooves beating the ground from the rumble. *Bada-DUM, bada-DUM, bada-DUM.*

It looked like the race was over as the leader, Lady Pecan, had a two-length lead over our filly. But Joe kicked his heels into Killer Graces' side, and the horse surged. Just as they came around to the final stretch, she had caught up and was dead even with Lady Pecan, one hundred yards to the finish.

"You've got this Steve-O!" yelled my friend.

The din was furious now, but I was even louder. With a last burst of energy, Killer Graces pulled ahead by a nose, then further,

further, and bolted past the cameras at the finish line. The crowd was out of its mind as the underdog pulled out a true underdog victory. I emitted a huge yell, feeling like the victor even though I was in the stands for the whole thing.

"Ahhh, come on," the leather man said as he crumpled his receipt.

I waved my badge and rushed through the security fence down to the track, shaking hands with everyone I passed, whether they were on our team or not.

A TV crew asked me for an interview. Afterward, I went over to the Winner's Circle and felt the eyes of the stadium on me as they flashed the official photo with our horse. I was beaming. Today, I wasn't just that sick guy anymore. Now I was really someone.

\* \* \*

After that race, I was completely hooked. I bought another horse. And another. And then another. And then before I really had time to stop and think about it, I was part owner of twelve horses. I couldn't even keep track of all of their names or the races they were running in.

Jen and I used the money from Killer Graces' winnings as a deposit to buy a house in Lake Tahoe with another family. When we told now-five-year-old Mia, she jumped up and down and yelled *"SNOOOOW!"* She had been watching a lot of Christmas specials. I felt proud that I could finally give her what I always felt she deserved.

I won a lot of races, and trainers started to notice, while other owners called me a mensch. I got interviewed by more TV stations in the winner's circle, and people at the track started to recognize me.

The racetrack started to feel like a home away from home. Every Saturday for six months, I would go down to Golden Gate

Fields in Berkeley at 1 p.m. and spend all day there. I'd sit for hours drinking at the Paddock bar, basically in the equivalent of a mall's food court on the lower level of the racetrack, meeting new people and building the myth of Steve.

Different groups who didn't frequent the track would come in on the weekend nights. That gave me my chance to shine.

"Did you guys win?" I said to a couple around my age sitting next to me one night.

The guy looked over at me, his cheeks already red from several drinks at the bar. "Lost a hundred," he said.

"Hundred and ten," his wife corrected. She swung her head over his way. "He's bad luck."

"And you're no good luck charm yourself," he replied, then asked me, "How'd you do today?"

"Lost a couple of bucks, lost more than a couple races," I said. "I own some of the horses that raced today."

His posture stiffened a little at that. "That right? How long you been an owner?"

"About a year now."

"And how'd you get into that?"

*Showtime.* I told them my story: the cancer, the surgeries, the chemo, the pills. I loved taking people on a ride through my story, watching their expressions change in shock, horror and ultimately amazement at what I had been through.

Then, the inevitable question. "How do you drink booze?" It was the guy, whose name was Russ, who asked it.

"Just like this," I said and pounded the shot of tequila on the bar. "Drink a little less, get a little drunker. Win-win."

They laughed at that, and I continued my story.

"I can't believe everything you've been through," the woman said.

It felt good to hear. I never got tired of it. *You're a survivor. An inspiration. Amazing.* The feeling was fleeting, always dissipating before I would ever even get home, but even a fleeting feeling is a good one.

Right on cue, my cell phone vibrated on the bar. It was Jennifer, and it was also somehow 10 p.m. and dark outside.

*When u coming home?*

*I'll be back in an hour.*

*Ok. Mia's asleep. Try to be quiet this time.*

*Ok.*

"How 'bout another shot then, my man?" Russ asked me.

"Can't say no to that."

An hour turned into two as we sat at the bar telling stories, then moved to another bar in Berkeley. Before I knew it, it was 2 a.m. I was in no shape to drive, so I called a cab that ended up costing a hundred dollars.

When I got home, I crept inside, past the toys lying all over the living room floor, praying I wouldn't wake Jennifer up for her to see what time it was.

Finally, I got to our room and slowly creaked the door open. Jennifer was curled up against Mia, who was sleeping in my spot. Neither one of them moved as I stood in the doorway.

I felt a drunken pang of jealousy as I thought something I had never previously considered: *She's trying to take my daughter away from me, to make Mia hers, not ours.*

I closed the door and went out on the deck, my mood now soured, and poured another glass of wine to end the night. I drank it slowly, and the quiet of the hillside enveloped me. Suddenly, a tentative *chirp, chirp, chirp* came from the bushes nearby. I cursed. Back before I had gotten cancer, when I would have friends over and we would party until the sun rose, the chirping of the waking birds in those bushes signaled that the sun was going to rise in an hour. It was always an unwelcome alarm back to reality.

I told the birds to go screw themselves and went to the guest bedroom, plopping down on the too-soft bed and falling immediately into a dreamless sleep.

\* \* \*

A door opened, then shut.

Jen's voice: "Blow."

I opened my eyes and oriented myself. The sun was shining through the windows in the guest bedroom, and a black object with a clear tip was close to my face. I had to go cross-eyed to see what it was.

A Breathalyzer.

"Are you serious?" I said. "You want me to blow into that? Good fucking morning."

Her lip was quivering. "Yes, I want you to blow into it. I know when you got home last night."

I hardly recognized the look on her face. Disgust? Hatred? She was looking at me like she had just found a stranger sleeping in her house. *This is exactly why I go to the racetrack every weekend,* I thought.

I considered arguing, but it didn't seem like she was up for it. I put my lips on the breathalyzer and looked up at her, hoping she would feel bad about what she was putting me through. This wasn't how a grown man was supposed to be treated. Fuck her.

I blew for several seconds until my head started throbbing. The machine beeped and displayed *ERROR.*

"Do it again."

"Come on, Jennifer. I'm not drunk."

"Do it again, Steve."

Her face was hard, unwavering. She was already dressed and had her shoes on. I wondered momentarily what time it was. It was probably already close to noon.

I inhaled deeply this time and blew hard into the machine. It beeped and clicked, unfortunately functioning correctly this time.

Jen pulled it out of my mouth forcefully and looked at it, then flashed a disgusted face. "I can't fucking believe this," she said as she showed me the number—0.08. "This is just absolutely ridiculous."

I felt like I was back in high school and my mom had caught me sneaking out.

"Jennifer, listen, just,—"

"No. No 'just'. You're completely out of control." She was yelling now.

"I'm not out of control. I just overdid it a little bit last night."

"Overdid it? You've been overdoing it every weekend for months. You're not in college anymore."

"Fucking sue me that I want to go out and have some fun after living through a year of hell."

"Oh, please. Coming out of a year of hell just to piss away your second chance at life."

"I'm just never supposed to have fun again?"

"You're still in *remission* from *cancer*, Steve. It could come back. You have to take care of yourself, for your life. For your *daughter's* life."

I got small. "Okay, please, just ... stop yelling. Mia's going to hear this. I'm sorry."

"I'm assuming—I'm hoping—you left your car in the East Bay. How are you planning on going to get it?"

"Well, since I just woke up ten seconds ago, I hadn't thought that far ahead."

"Better start thinking about it, or you're stuck here all day. Mia and I are going to the store." She stormed out of the room and slammed the door.

I laid my head, already throbbing, back down on my pillow. *Why the hell did she get so pissed? It's not like I'm coming home from work getting plastered. It's the goddamn weekend.*

In my mind, she couldn't have been more wrong—this *was* life. This was everything I had been missing for the past two years. I could have a few drinks and then have fun again. I could be social. Without alcohol, I couldn't get myself to eat enough food to be a real, functioning person. I would drop into a days-long funk. Did she want me to be *that* way, instead?

I lay in bed for half an hour, paralyzed by the hangover that I knew was coming. Then, I said fuck it, got up and took a taxi back to the racetrack for the Sunday races. No one there judged me for drinking, like Jen did. They cheered me on and called me things like *hero* and *inspiration.*

In the cab ride over to Berkeley, I pulled out my phone and logged into Facebook. I went to Tanya's profile. Her main picture showed her, tanned and with black hair, smiling in a close-up with her kids. I felt jealous looking at that photo.

I sent her a message: *Got in another fight with Jen. I just don't know how to fix this.*

The less I felt like I could talk to Jen, the more I had turned to Tanya as a confidante. She had the unique perspective of only really knowing me in high school and not during the terrible post-cancer times. I felt like we could talk without any of that baggage getting in the way.

She replied within a minute: *You can still fix it. You just have to be open and honest. You have to communicate.*

Usually her advice was really helpful, but this time it wasn't hitting home. The fights between Jen and me had become an all-encompassing cycle. Jen was upset by my behavior, which made her react in a frustrated way when I wasn't being the husband or the father I was supposed to be. Which then caused me to retreat further away from her, exacerbating the issue and making her more frustrated. It all reinforced itself.

The cab pulled up to the racetrack. I got out, put on my best smile and walked inside of the place where I was somebody.

# CHAPTER
# FOURTEEN

 Mia stood perched on a rock eight feet above a river. She looked down and took a tentative step forward. Just like me when I was her age, she was willing to try anything, and she was good at everything.

We had taken a short hike here from our condo in Cabo San Lucas at the southern tip of Baja in Mexico. We came here every summer, bringing along friends and family and whoever else wanted to come. This time, we came with a few of my friends and their families, who were all back at the villa. Our therapist had recommended we do more things as a family, so Jen, Mia and I took a hike together.

I stood behind Mia, encouraging her to jump in.

"You're going to love it!" I said. "The water feels so cold down there."

"I don't want cold!"

"Trust me. Do you want me to go first?"

She nodded and backed away. I approached the edge and feigned a jump. Mia giggled behind me. I turned around and smiled at her, then jumped off and did a backflip as I crashed into the cold water below.

"Woah! That was so cool daddy!"

"You can do that too, Mia!" I yelled over the sound of the waterfall nearby.

With that, she jumped right into the water, screeching on the way down.

"Cold, cold, cold!" she said as she came up. She paddled over to me and wrapped herself around my neck.

"You'll love it in a minute. Just wait." I spun her around in the water.

"It's all tingly."

I spotted Jen on the rocks nearby, leaning on her elbows in a bathing suit.

"Wave to mommy."

She screamed: "HI MOMMY!"

"Right in my ear!"

Jen smiled and waved back.

"Alright, now go back up and jump again! I want to see a flip."

She went back again and again, and by her fifth jump she could do a slightly sideways version of a flip. I smiled. She always amazed me.

We hiked back to the villa by sundown and met up with everyone for drinks and dinner. The kids went downstairs to the playroom, while the adults had drinks and got rowdy. These vacations were a reprieve from real life, where it felt like it was acceptable to be drinking any time, any day. Even Jen didn't look at me with side-eyes during these trips.

But that was the big deception. We were great at having fun during those escapes, but when reality hit, we just weren't a good team. When we got back home, into the humdrum of regular life, the continued digs at my drinking picked back up. I retreated again to the racetrack, while she immersed herself in her work.

By 2012, almost three years after I had quit the opiates, Jennifer and I were basically living separate lives, our marriage hanging on by a thread. Jen took Mia on little girl field trips around town, which came to far outnumber any time we spent together as a family.

I flew wherever the wind blew me. I started to get into harder partying and was coming home later on more nights. I left my credit cards all over the place, then would cancel them instead of facing the shame of closing out my tab the next day. I spent less time hanging out with my closest friends, opting instead for the random people at the bar who would heap fawning praise on me for my status as a survivor. It was the same, and yet it was also something new every night. As the walls started to close in around me at home, I became a nomad. I was a fricking mess.

The only times I started to look forward to home was when I would get Mia to myself. One night, we had a dance recital for play-time. Mia ran to Jen's closet and pulled out a pair of the highest heels she could find. Then she clomped around on the tile while I clapped and cheered her on. I turned the speakers on loud, and we danced in our socks together.

"Daddy," she said when we stopped to catch our breath. "Why don't we play more often?"

"What do you mean, sweetie?"

"You always have a headache."

She had picked up on so much more than I expected. "Oh. It's just, daddy sometimes has issues from when he was sick a while ago. He still feels it sometimes."

She looked uncertain. "Well maybe I can make it better!"

I laughed. "Okay, baby. Next time, just give me a kiss on the forehead. Let's see it." I leaned my head down, and she came over and gave me a peck.

"No, no, MUCH bigger."

This time, she laughed and ran up, giving me a big, wet *MWWWWAAAAH* on the head.

"There we go!"

That night, it began to occur to me that maybe it wasn't just Jen keeping me away from raising my daughter. Maybe I was doing it myself.

* * *

I reached the winter of that year thinking I could still handle myself, until the first Friday of December.

That day was our company Christmas party. After work, everyone in the office hit the bars downtown, and I drank more cocktails than anyone. One of my co-workers commented: "You can really knock 'em back."

"Pretty impressive for a guy with no stomach, right?"

I went with a group of coworkers to other clubs and, finally, a strip club on Columbus Avenue. Eventually, I found myself sitting alone in the strip club, without any of my coworkers. A place like that suddenly becomes extremely depressing when you're not with other people. I knew I couldn't drive home, so I was stranded in the city.

I stumbled back to my office's parking garage several blocks away and climbed into the back of my SUV, curling up on the back seat.

After an indeterminable amount of time, I woke up with my back aching, still in my suit from the workday. I felt so pathetic. I had a family back home, and instead of going to spend time with them, instead of *wanting* to spend time with them during the holiday season, I wanted to be in the city, getting drunk with co-workers. *What the fuck is wrong with me? What am I doing?*

I checked my watch: 8 a.m. I climbed over the center console and into the driver's seat, already dreading the moment I would enter the house, still dressed up from yesterday, reeking of booze.

When I got home, Jen was making breakfast. She shot a glare at me. Mia looked confused at the breakfast table.

"Are you going to work, daddy?"

I withered. "No, sweetie." I tried to think of an excuse, an explanation for why I was dressed up. But all that came out was: "No. Not today."

"Daddy just needs to get changed," Jen said. "And maybe go lie down."

"Just for a little bit," I responded. "Maybe we can do something fun today."

"Mia and I are going to the mall to see Santa," Jen said.

I looked at her, hurt, then turned away with tears in my eyes and headed to our room.

I sat in bed, agonizing over what I had done. What I was *still* doing. The path I was taking, the meaninglessness of my experiences while the most important person in my life was growing up without me. This was it. I had to start doing something different.

Later that evening, I approached Jen in the living room.

"Can we talk?" I asked.

She nodded without speaking.

"I know I have a problem, and I want to get better. So, I'm going to check in for a 30-day rehab program. I can check in tomorrow."

She looked like she was waiting for me to say I was kidding. I held my eyes on hers.

"Good," she said, then got up and walked away.

\* \* \*

Jen drove me to Serenity Rehab Center the next day. We stayed silent in the car most of the way. There was no talk about our future. It was starting to seem like we didn't really have a future after rehab.

"Why are you still with me?" I asked.

She sat with her lips pursed long enough that I gave up on getting an answer.

"We have a six-year-old daughter together."

So that was it. This marriage was now just a stage set for Mia. We didn't say much after that. I grabbed my duffel bag when we pulled up, and Jen made no motion to get out. We said a curt goodbye through the open window.

When I walked in, the staff took away all of my belongings — wallet, cell phone, keys — and sent me to a detox room. One of the people at the facility told me it was the same room where Jerry Garcia from the Grateful Dead died. I wondered if there would be a plaque on the wall to commemorate the morbid association, but I was disappointed.

The detox itself wasn't too bad and was miles easier than my detox from opiates. I was hot and sweaty for a couple of days before getting admitted into the regular part of the facility to attend one AA meeting after another. It was all interesting and enlightening at first, but I got bored quickly of surrendering to a higher power. Whatever the hell that meant.

Two weeks later, it was December 23rd, and I felt like a complete loser at the thought of missing the holidays with Mia. I didn't think I needed to be here anymore. *Other* people might need this to get sober, but I didn't. I could get all the results I needed at home.

I missed an AA meeting, and when a counselor came to my room to check on me, I got angry and yelled at him to leave me the fuck alone.

Finally, I got sent to a meeting with the head counselor.

"Why do I still have to be here?" I asked him.

He leaned back in his chair. "You don't. If you think you've gotten everything you're going to get out of this, you can go. Just don't have that first drink and go to all the meetings you can."

So that was it. Freedom. All I had to do was ask, and, I suppose, cause a scene. Maybe the only reason they were letting me go was because I was a problem.

I packed my bags and left rehab the next day, riding home with Jen. She was upset and suspicious, but she eventually softened and seemed relieved I was there for Christmas, for Mia's sake.

"This Steve is the one who's here to stay," I said.

Of course, I hadn't even convinced myself of that fact, and my first slip-up was just one week later, at a New Year's Eve party. I just couldn't have fun sipping on a soda water while everyone else was tanked, belting out anthems. I snuck off into a bathroom with a bottle of vodka and took a couple of small shots to take the edge off. The fact that it was covert, that I was doing something I wasn't supposed to, made it even more exciting as I blended in with the crowd. I didn't get drunk that night, but the door was back wide open.

A few weeks later, Jen and I were having dinner with another family in Lake Tahoe when I ordered a glass of Cabernet Sauvignon, my first drink in public since getting out of rehab. I tried to do it nonchalantly, saying, "I'll just have a ... Cabernet," but I also knew the reaction this was going to get. Jen glared at me, and our dinner-mates seemed to suck in a deep breath and hold it.

"Really?" Jen said.

"Yeah. It's okay, I'm good."

And it was fine. I did control it ... that night. I had just two glasses of wine and went to bed. Jen and I didn't talk about it.

Back home, I went to Tanya again on Facebook Messenger, confiding in her that I had a few drinks.

She replied quickly. *At least you're being honest about it. I think you're more aware of yourself than most people. It's only a few drinks, but I do think you have to be careful.*

*Yeah. I want to say that I can handle it, but I also know that I'm not always as perfect at handling things as I think.*

*I think you're doing your best, given everything you've been through.*

I asked her what I should do about Jen.

*I wish I could help. I'm thinking about leaving my fiancé. I'm not sure I'm the best to come to for advice on relationships.*

I wanted to show empathy, but more than anything, I felt excited. In the process of leaning on Tanya for support all this time, it had started to feel like she was the only person I could talk to. I could say to her that I was concerned about my drinking, and just have her hear me without being afraid she was going to judge me for it.

*Really? Sorry to hear that. But honestly, I could tell you were too good for him.*

*Thanks. You're not bad yourself ;)*

I re-read that last message thirty times. I wasn't sure the last time someone had said something like that to me. People told me I was a hero, a survivor, but no one told me that right here, right now, I was *attractive*. I logged out of Facebook and closed the computer.

\* \* \*

I was sitting on my couch one Saturday morning in February when my phone started buzzing. The caller ID said P.J. Gallaway. I looked at the phone and let it ring a few times. Over the past several months, I had tried to reach out to P.J. I called him when he reached his five-year survival milestone, and then I called again when I reached my own three months later. But each time I got his voicemail. Then, out of the blue, I would get emails from him asking for donations to support his Gastric Cancer Foundation. I always gave money, but it started to feel like I was being used. The distance between us had grown.

I answered the phone. It wasn't P.J.'s voice.

"Hi, Steve. It's Mindy, P.J.'s wife." She sounded weary.

*Oh, God.* I thought I knew what was coming.

"I'm calling because—because I just wanted to let you know that P.J. passed away." My mouth fell open in shocked silence as she quietly whimpered for a few seconds. "I wanted to let you know in case you want to come to the service."

"Oh my god. Wha- what happened?"

She told me his cancer had returned, and his body couldn't fight it anymore. I checked the date on my phone: February 26, 2013. He had beaten that five-year survival rate: *15 percent*. But what did that milestone even matter when he died six months later?

I couldn't fathom it. He had lived his life perfectly—he ate right, he exercised, he was spiritual, he loved his family—while I was doing everything possible to destroy my body. How could he die while I stayed alive? It seemed ... impossible.

It hit me that the one guiding light I had, who proved I could survive cancer and its aftermath, was now gone. By the quick, irrational calculation I did in my head, I had about three months to live.

"Thanks for letting me know, Mindy," I said, realizing I had left her on the line. "I'll be at the service. I hope you and the kids are holding up okay."

Jen overheard me on the phone and asked what happened after I hung up.

"It was P.J. Galloway's wife. He died."

"Oh. Oh no, that's so sad."

"Yeah."

"Those poor kids."

"Yeah." I didn't want to be around her for this moment. It didn't even seem to occur to her what *I* might be feeling because of this news. I went downstairs to be alone.

For some people, this might be the come-to-Jesus, clean-up-your-act moment. It wasn't for me. After hearing about what happened to P.J., I drank nonstop, poisoning my already-broken body. Over the next month, I spiraled out of control, going to the ER multiple times in from alcohol-related issues.

I stayed in San Francisco after work and went to clubs, then slept in my car regularly. When I was home, I would sneak off to message Tanya. Our conversations were now growing more explicit. Jennifer saw how much I was on my phone and got suspicious. She asked the only computer whiz in our house, Mia, to break into my phone and found the messages I had shared with Tanya.

Jen told me to sleep in the guest bedroom. I took that as a directive to sleep there every night, while Mia slept in our room with Jen. I felt more and more like I was losing control of my family.

We talked about divorce like it was now an inevitability. We got far enough to actually start discussing who would have Mia on the weekends.

Even my friends, many of whom still drank every weekend, started to raise the issue with me. When I called one of my best friends, Rick, from a bar one night, trying to get him involved in some random conversation I was having with a person sitting next to me, he immediately put a stop to it.

"Dude, I'm not sure what to do with you, Steve," Rick said. "You need to get some help."

I wrote him off and just tried to continue distracting myself. I made plans with Tanya to meet up for the Kentucky Derby in May.

One evening, I brought Mia to a restaurant in Tiburon, where we met with another family for dinner. I drank more wine than everyone else at the table and before too long I had to ask the family for a ride home. I tried to be subtle as to why daddy couldn't drive, but Mia had a look on her face that told me on a certain level she knew what was going on.

The next morning, I woke up in the guest room at 3 a.m. with a burning feeling in my stomach. Trying to head off the shame of how I had acted at dinner, I went straight to the wine cellar, then out to the back patio with two bottles of wine. I sat there in misery, knowing that I was really going to die this time, whether it was the cancer coming back like it did for P.J. or if it was me doing it to myself.

By the time the birds chirped to signal the sunrise, I had drunk both bottles. I went inside, curled up on the floor in the kitchen and prayed out loud for help—from God, from whoever.

I had a flash to my possible future: Mia, as a teenager, resenting her drunk of a father who she never sees anymore. Even when that father reaches out to apologize, to say how much of a hard time he was going through, to blame the C-word, she'd barely listen, knowing he had made a million choices to put himself in this situation. That the cancer was all an excuse.

If I wanted to get out of this, if I wanted to avoid that future and have Mia remember her father as anything but a drunk, I needed to get real help. I needed to stop pretending I could handle this all on my own.

I got up off the floor and started texting friends, family, anyone who could find me an open rehab facility. A friend found a place in Sonoma County, and I asked Jennifer if she could take me that day.

"Fuck no, you're on your own," she said as she was making breakfast.

I begged her, crying in the kitchen, and finally she agreed.

"I swear, it'll be the last thing I ever ask you to do for me," I said.

I went into Mia's room and woke her up. She looked at me with sleepy, confused eyes.

"Hey, sweetie. Daddy has to go on a trip today."

"A trip? Where are you going?"

"To the forest. I'm going on a retreat."

"For how long?"

I didn't want to say it, but I knew I couldn't lie to her. "A month."

"That's so long!"

"I know. But when I get back, we're going to have extra daddy and Mia time."

"You promise?"

"Yes, I promise."

I kissed her and gently pulled her door closed.

This time, I told myself, a month was really going to be a month, no matter how hard it was.

# CHAPTER

# FIFTEEN

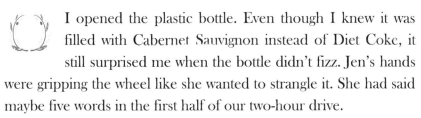I opened the plastic bottle. Even though I knew it was filled with Cabernet Sauvignon instead of Diet Coke, it still surprised me when the bottle didn't fizz. Jen's hands were gripping the wheel like she wanted to strangle it. She had said maybe five words in the first half of our two-hour drive.

For this round of rehab, we were heading to Alpine Acres, which lay in a redwood forest in Sonoma County. On the way over, while guzzling the last bit of alcohol I'd ever be able to drink, I sneakily texted Tanya, who was saved in my phone as Dave.

*I'm really sorry, but I won't be able to do the Derby. I'm heading to rehab.*

Then, I called my boss and told her where I was going, too. I thought of lying but figured the truth was the only way forward. Not to mention that I was already drunk at 10 a.m., so I was feeling very honest.

My phone buzzed, a message from "Dave."

*Oh my god. You have no idea how glad I am to hear that. Because I wasn't even planning on going to the Derby. I was planning an intervention for you.*

I sighed audibly, and Jen looked over briefly before turning back to the road.

We pulled onto a gravel path that led to a dark wood building with vistas of rolling green hills in all directions.

I got out and tried to give Jennifer a hug goodbye. She lent me one arm for the hug.

"I just hope you take it seriously and get the help you need."

"I'm going to be a different man the next time you see me." I tried my best to say it without slurring any of my words.

"Well, don't count on seeing me anytime soon. You're going to get a letter from my attorney."

I walked away without saying anything. So, this was what it was all coming down to: lawyers, motions in court, *custody arrangements*. It was just strange that it came with such a whimper, not an explosion.

Approaching the front door, I pushed my shoulders back and blanketed myself in the defense mechanism I always used when thrust into an uncomfortable situation: I became the jokester.

"I swear I don't have wine teeth, I just had cancer," I said to the humorless, stout woman at the front desk. I scrawled an illegible signature on the intake form, laughing at how hilarious I was. I figured I'd take it more seriously when I sobered up, but for now I could have a little fun.

After my first stint in rehab, I knew the deal. I stuffed my personal phone in my sock and kept my business phone in my pocket. When the attendant asked me to hand over my phone, I gave them the business one. I didn't want to be completely disconnected from the outside world.

Then I went inside, where some of the residents were playing ping-pong. I filled myself with the run-this-place mentality that comes with stepping into an unknown location while drunk and immediately challenged the winner to a game.

"We've got a wet one over here," said a bald, tattooed guy. The rest laughed and eyed me suspiciously. I won my first four games and proclaimed that I was the King of Rehab. Then, as the alcohol wore off, I started missing shots all over the place, and the other guys laughed at me. It started to sink in that I wouldn't be able to escape and get a drink. My hands started to shake, and my breath quickened. Eventually I had to sit down, then lie down.

"He looks ready for the sweat lodge," said the tattooed guy.

The attendants gave me some Valium and then showed me to the detox room, where I lay for two days next to a moaning mailman, while sweating through a couple layers of sheets every night.

Finally, on the evening of the third day, they put me in a regular room with two guys named Andy and Chad.

"Made it out of the sweats?" Chad asked.

"Brutal," I replied.

"What are you here for?" Andy asked me. He looked at my arms, the veins pulsing out of my tiny biceps. "Meth? *Herr-on?*"

"Oh, god. No. I mean, I've done a lot, but—yeah. Not that." I knew I was being awkward, and there was a strong possibility these guys were here for just those things.

Andy had a short, jolting laugh that started and stopped on a dime. *HA-ha.* "Well, then what?"

"Booze, mostly."

Andy smiled but held the laugh in. "Amazes me that people can get this fucked over by booze, when there're so many better highs waiting just around the corner."

"Well, what are you here for?" I asked him.

"Name it, I'd say I'm here for it."

Andy told me he was a musician, and he was twenty-seven. He joked about how Hendrix and Cobain and all the other musicians died at that age and said he was going to be different. He was going to see twenty-eight.

He had signed a $250,000 record deal with a major label before the heroin and coke habit took him over. Then he backed out of the deal over a disagreement. Bills started to pile up, and production went down the drain.

"My manager made me come here," he said. It was one of the few sentences he hadn't punctuated with that short laugh.

Chad, who was closer in age to me and had a laid-back surfer vibe that had characterized everyone I met in San Diego, got into trouble after his wife asked for a divorce. He drove his 4Runner onto the freeway and floored the gas, hoping to smash into a retaining wall. Jesus didn't take the wheel, but He blew up Chad's engine, bringing the car to a safe stop in the middle of the highway. Chad checked into rehab a few days later.

"Shit," I said. "Well, I guess I'm in a similar boat to you. I think I'll be getting divorce papers while I'm in here."

"So did your wife make you come here?" Andy said.

I thought for a while. I thought of the four-month bender that ended with me praying on the floor of the kitchen. I thought of Jen, of the yelling and the accusations, and started to feel all the anger bubble up. But then I thought of how many of the accusations were true.

"I guess I forced myself."

He nodded. "Profound, man."

I could tell early on that Andy and I were kindred spirits. Neither one of us had any inhibitions. For him, that was because everyone in his life licked his boots. Anytime he picked up a guitar, people came out of the woodwork to sit and listen. Everyone told him how famous he was going to be.

For me, that was because I thought I had seen everything in life, that I had been through the wringer enough not to worry about whether people thought I was an idiot.

As I settled into bed that night, listening to the crickets chirping outside the windows, I felt strangely relieved to be here. It was in my hands to be sober, but at the same time I could let go of control and just be present. I thought to myself that, after all I had put everyone through, this would be the time I would really embrace this strange place I was in and make lasting changes. As I was thinking of these things, I heard Chad talking in his sleep, saying over and over again: "It's all gooooood." It was soothing.

That night, I dreamt of Mia dancing in her socks, sliding across the room with wiggly legs to the sound of "Cut loose ... Footloose!" I kept up with her on the living room floor, pumping my arms as I crossed the room. My body felt strangely normal. Nothing felt missing.

In the dream, I went over to the stereo and slowly turned the dial, boosting the music louder and louder as Mia looked at me approvingly. She giggled and waved her head around, her snowy blonde hair flowing through the air. I was awestruck at how much she looked like me as a child. She had become the most beautiful six-year-old girl, and I felt so much love for her that my head started to spin.

The noodling *benene, nenene* guitar solo came, and I mimicked a guitar lick. She copied me and then fell to the ground laughing.

She got up out of breath and stopped dancing, then yelled something that was drowned out by the music.

"What?" I said.

"You ru—" Again the music was too loud.

I got closer to her and looked at her mouth. "One more time, baby girl," I said in a mock-Elvis voice.

"You ruined everything!"

I took a step back. Her smile had vanished. In its place, her brows were furrowed, and her lip curled down. Suddenly the music was a distorted version of itself, the guitars all wrong, the drums off-beat.

"Mi—Mia, what do you mean?"

She shrieked. "It's all your FAULT!"

I woke up to the heavy thumping of footsteps on hardwood floor. For a few moments, I was confused, the blanket feeling too light, the bed too stiff. I wondered where Mia was.

A door opened behind me, and a man's voice came through. "Breakfast," he said.

I blinked and looked around.

*Oh, right,* I thought. *Rehab.*

The early morning sun had already over brightened the bleach-white walls, which were decorated with framed stock image photos discussing MOTIVATION and POWER.

"Get up, guys," a voice from the doorway said.

I looked over to see David, the grouchy floor supervisor, wearing a polo shirt tucked into khakis. He was in his fifties but dressed like a kid in prep school.

Andy leaned up against the wall on the other side of the room. His pompadour, usually perfectly gelled, was tousled into a rat's nest and he emitted a low growl as he stretched. He looked at me for a second and smacked his lips.

"Come on, let's get moving," David said.

"Where's the fire?" Andy responded. "Are we prisoners?" He looked at me with a grin.

David sighed wearily. He had no patience for Andy's antics, which only seemed to make Andy double down. "Just get up."

Andy bolted up and strode to the end of the room in an over-eager walk, looking at me the whole way as he bobbed up and down. I laughed as I stood up.

The fog that had clouded my head since I had stepped in the front door, completely plastered three days earlier, had finally faded. I didn't feel the compulsive need to find the nearest bottle.

We walked to the dining hall, a tall room with four communal benches in the middle and impressionistic paintings lining the walls.

The rustic wooden furniture looked like it had been hacked out of one of the trees on the grounds. The faded floorboards creaked loudly enough for people in the next room to hear every footstep.

A couple dozen people were separated into different eating groups, like in high school. Sitting at one table and talking the loudest were the college-aged kids, tattooed, pale and thin, the kinds who started snorting Xanax at fourteen, toyed with OxyContin, and then finally realized that heroin was cheaper and easier to get.

In another group were the senior citizens, guys in their fifties and sixties whose lives revolved around alcohol. They were grumpy and prone to talking like priests, except quoting the Twelve Steps and not the Bible.

Sitting on the periphery were the meth addicts, easily the scariest and most unpredictable of the bunch, whose withdrawals involved a lot of screaming and itching.

Then there were the middle-aged ones who had made a living for themselves but still clearly fucked up royally somewhere along the way. Booze mixed with cocaine and maybe some ecstasy were our vices of choice. This group included me and Chad.

"You know you talk in your sleep?" I told Chad when we sat down. "You kept saying: 'It's all goooood!' What's so damn good, Chad?"

"Just thinking about your wife." He smiled.

"Alright, I set you up for that."

The woman who worked the front desk came into the dining hall. "Melen? Steve Melen?"

I raised my hand and she delivered an envelope for me. It was from an attorney's office in San Francisco. I opened it and read the first line. PETITION FOR DIVORCE.

Jen wasn't bluffing. This was real. It was over. We were going to raise Mia as divorced parents.

Looking over my shoulder, Chad patted my back.

"Jesus," I said. "I mean, I knew it was coming. But seeing it, it's just different. Like, it's really over. There's no saving it."

"That feeling is the worst part, trust me. It'll get better."

Another supervisor whose name I didn't know, called from the door, "Five minutes left for breakfast, then group session."

"What do we do in group session?" I asked Chad.

"You get with like eight people and talk about your feelings and shit."

"Oh." My vision went blurry as I felt a wave of anxiety come over me.

In college I developed an extreme aversion toward group situations that I have no control over. My first day of class freshman year, as the teacher was going around the room doing icebreakers, I literally stood up and walked out of the classroom, my cheeks on fire, rather than introducing myself. That anxiety continued and ramped up through my twenties, until my therapist had to put me on some sort of Prozac after I had a panic attack at work. It didn't stop me from becoming successful in high-intensity environments, but some situations triggered that claustrophobia.

We were shepherded to a smaller, sparsely decorated room that was several degrees too cold. I was apprehensive as I approached the circle of metal chairs in the middle, unsure if there was a specific one I should take. When I sat, my knees were almost touching the people on either side of me. I didn't really know any of the people in there. My hands were shaking. I tried to remember what my therapist told me. *None of this matters, it's all in my head. None of this matters. It's all in my head. None of this matters.*

A supervisor named Dan sat down to lead the group. His short-sleeved shirt revealed the old track marks on his arms. I barely paid any attention to the reading he opened the class with.

As if on cue, he looked straight at me. "We've got someone new in our group today."

Blood rushed to my head, and my vision blurred again.

"Steve, is it? Why don't you tell us about yourself and how you got here?"

I laughed nervously and swallowed. "How much time do you have?"

"As much time as you need," he said.

Everyone was looking at me.

I shifted in my seat. "Well, I'm not really sure where to start my story. I feel like I could start in a million places. I had stomach cancer, and I had to get several of my organs removed."

I surveyed the room to gauge the faces around me. I thought I'd be able to get them on my side quickly, to get the tears flowing. But they weren't impressed. They looked stoic—these people had been through the wringer, too. I was on my heels.

"That was more than five years ago. And I only had a fifteen percent chance of surviving those five years. I've made it this far, but things in my personal life, with my wife, have sort of ...bubbled up."

"How have they bubbled up?"

"Well, my wife, she just wanted to yell at me all the time. And my daughter — Jen was pulling her away from me. They were always doing things together, leaving me out."

A beer-bellied guy with a handlebar mustache sitting across the room chimed in. "I know about that," he said.

"And what were you doing to contribute to those issues 'bubbling up?'" Dan asked.

The walls started to feel like they were closing in. "Don't worry, I get it. I've been to therapy. I was distancing. I hung out at the racetrack a lot. I got drunk a lot. Chasing something more exciting. But can you blame me for wanting to have some fun after years of hell?"

"You're minimizing it," Dan said.

"I'm not minimizing anything."

"Yes, you are," he said, and he stared at me for several seconds. "You think you already know everything we're going to go over in here. You think you're the smartest guy in the room."

I stared back at him, vaguely wanting to hit him, while the whole room looked at me. I was silent.

"Did you try to mend things with your wife?" he asked.

I tried to choose my words carefully. "Well, it was hard to do that when my wife would wake me up with a Breathalyzer test. She just wanted to yell at me all the time. She didn't want to contribute anything positive. She just told me how much of a fuck-up I was."

"Mm," he said, nodding slowly. "But you didn't want to see your daughter more? Wouldn't it have been better to work on things, just for her?"

I looked around at the ten other people in the room. Brittany, an eighteen-year-old girl who came in with a dull haze from heroin use, was sitting in her chair, nodding as if to say, *We all get it, why don't you?*

"I'm telling you, I did what I did because I couldn't stand to be around my house anymore. When every time Jen would see me meant she was yelling at me, I just couldn't fucking bear it."

I could see some of the others in the group start to roll their eyes and groan softly, and two people whispered something to each other.

Dan broke the silence. "I can't help you right now. I can't help you because if you want to get better, you're going to have to work with us, and you're going to have to be honest. You'll have to be honest with me and stop BS-ing yourself."

"No, you don't understand," I went on, starting to panic. "You don't know the shit she put me through. You don't get it."

"Actually, we do get it. You're not better or worse than anyone else in here."

"Alright, fine." I crossed my arms and closed myself off.

"I'd encourage you to listen to other people's stories today," Dan said.

"Sure. Whatever."

I resolved that I would just stare at the clock for the next hour until it was over. But as people shared their stories, I couldn't help but listen. One guy talked about his dad dying, and a woman said her spouse cheated on her, while a third person had a near-death experience. It was clear that everyone who spoke had their own unique trauma that led them to drinking, and each one of those stories was completely real to the person who experienced it.

Before long, I realized that Dan was right. For so long, I had been trying to separate myself from other people, telling myself that my situation was different. But I wasn't special. Everyone had their story.

At the end of the session, Dan asked if anyone else had anything to say, and I raised my hand.

"I just wanted to say I'm sorry. I've been blaming my alcohol abuse on my cancer. I've been saying that because I went through that, I should be able to do whatever I want. That my wife and everyone else has no right to criticize me for my actions, when they haven't seen what I've seen, or been through what I went through. And I've damaged all of my relationships by doing that."

The group around me stayed quiet, nodding their heads.

"Thank you," Dan said. "Thank you for being honest. I have one more question for you. In some ways, do you think you wanted the cancer to come back?"

"What?"

"Would that have made things easier for you, if the cancer had just come back?"

I had to think. *Of course I didn't want it to come back, why would I want to die? But, then again, cancer was a permanent Get-Out-of-Jail-Free card.*

He went on before I could reply. "I think a little part of you does wish it had just come back. Because then nothing would have been your fault."

In that moment, I realized just how distant I had been from myself, like I was living life ten feet above my own head, just moving forward, not really seeing what was going on around me.

"I—I guess I'm ultimately here because I couldn't stand to fail them. I couldn't have the people in my life judging me. Saying, 'You came out of cancer, how could you now fucking kill yourself?' I ran away from everyone in my life." I started to cry.

The room was silent, without a chair creaking, and the counselor nodded his head.

"This whole time, your life has revolved around you. You've seen everything in the world through your own eyes, and because of that, you think that your interpretation is correct." He paused and looked around. "And that applies to everyone in this room, not just you."

I looked around at everyone nodding. Suddenly, I felt like I wasn't that different from anyone here. And that sameness felt surprisingly good. A huge weight, days' worth of self-guardedness, lifted from my shoulders. I closed my eyes.

Dan adjourned the session and handed me a leaflet that said *HUMILITY* in big letters on the front. "Humility is the humbling of yourself in service of others," it read.

I thought of those words, of the past four years, of how despite it all, I convinced myself that I was doing everything I could, that I was living my life the only way possible. I could never be wrong because I was a cancer patient. With Jennifer, with the friends who tried to tell me I needed help.

Late that afternoon, I walked down the stone pathway to a small lake that, judging by the cigarette butts and empty bottles, was the site for many of the banned activities at the rehab center. But it was still beautiful, with tiny ripples running over the surface of the blueish-brown water. I felt a breeze whistle through my hair, chilling my bones. Normally, this would send me running for a jacket, but for a few minutes, I just sat there and felt it. I savored the goosebumps on my body, then the slight warmth of the distant sun.

In that moment, I realized that all these years I had been trying to feel something, I really hadn't felt anything at all. I had always been trying to chase something else, to reclaim a bit of my past life, but what really was I trying to reclaim? I was the dog on the track, chasing the rabbit, never able to catch it. I hadn't sat in the moment and listened to what was going on around me.

I once thought that if I could get through cancer, I could get through anything else the world threw at me. How pathetic that I had dug myself into an even deeper hole, that I had let everyone who was counting on me down. My wife, my daughter, my friends, my family. I curled my knees up to my chest and cried for a long time, then thought about how all I wanted to do was hug Mia.

# CHAPTER
# SIXTEEN

By my third week in rehab, the uncontrollable urge to find a drink had faded. I settled into a routine and had begun to even enjoy my time there, in a sense. At night, Andy and I sat out on the deck playing guitar and making up stupid songs, like spelling out C-O-C-A-I-N-E to a swinging groove. We always had an audience, and our back-and-forth storytelling kept people enraptured.

Andy smoked like a chimney, and I acquired the habit through osmosis.

"Do you even have lungs?" Andy asked me the first time I bummed one from him.

I coughed when I inhaled it. "Maybe not. Hard to keep track anymore."

During the day, I attended one AA meeting after another and wrote mock letters to people I had wronged in the past. I wrote at least ten letters to Jen and thought about actually sending them, but I just couldn't do it.

But at night, when I pulled my cell phone out from under my pillow, I was reminded that life was still going on without me outside those walls. The unanswered emails and the missed appointments were piling up. And every day, new papers from Jennifer's lawyer screeched out of the front desk's fax machine. The office administrator had a knack for embarrassingly handing them to me at breakfast. *You've got divorce mail, bitch!*

The lawyer-y text of those letters was getting more aggressively lawyer-y as time went on, discussing STEVEN's mental state and addiction issues. Eventually one paper arrived screaming RELEASE OF CUSTODY OF CHILD, and I let out about twenty *fucks* when I read that headline.

The paper said that Jen would get full custody of Mia, and that I would be allowed only supervised visits. It felt like the kind of thing that an abusive husband would get. It didn't seem fair. But, in that moment, I fully understood just how much I had put Jen through, and I thought that I owed her everything. It felt like the only way we could have an amicable relationship and be functioning co-parents for Mia would be if I gave her whatever she wanted.

I signed the paper without any amendments, then gave it to the receptionist to fax back over. As soon as it finished faxing, though, I felt like I had made a mistake: Had I really thought through all the ramifications of what I was doing? What had I just given up?

With a week left in rehab, I went into a meeting with Dan, who was also my one-on-one counselor. His small office was framed by a big bookshelf with generic psychology lining the walls. His desk was scattered with all sorts of papers. Over the weeks, Dan and I had developed a good relationship. He talked straight and didn't put up with my bullshit, which I liked.

I told him about the divorce and custody agreement.

"I see. That was a very big thing you did there. What are you planning on doing when you get out of here?"

"I guess I'll go back home. But I don't know. I might have to move out and get an apartment."

"Mm. You may not want to hear this, but I think you should go live in a sober living environment. You need to be surrounded by a support system of people going through the same thing you are. Like what you have here."

"What? No way. I'd never be able to have my daughter visit if I did that. I can just get my own apartment in Tiburon and go to meetings."

"If you do that, you're throwing the last thirty days in the trash. You're not going to make it."

I puffed my chest out and said, "Hell, yes, I can make it, I'm Steve Melen, I survived cancer, motherfucker. What did you survive?"

Or something like that.

He clicked his tongue.

"A few months ago, I had a guy who was just like you."

"He sounds made up." I was messing with him, but he glared at me.

"We had a guy like you in here—I'll call him Kevin, for confidentiality and all that. Really successful. Financial type. He had a little bit more money than everyone else in here, and he walked around like it. Toward the end, Kevin says he's brand new, that he can go back home to his wife and kids. All that. So, he gets done with his thirty days and heads back home and is doing great for a while. Going well with his wife, playing with his kids."

"This is already different from me. I'm *divorced*, remember? My kid might not even be there."

"Just listen for a sec, okay? It's going great until he gets back into his old routine. Then he realizes that everything about his routine involved drinking: happy hours with co-workers, drinking lunches with clients, you know. So, he tries making different routines. He goes to night classes instead of bars, and plenty of AA meetings.

"But the problem is, on his way to and from work every day, he drives past his favorite bar, one of those Irish pubs that shows every Giants game. You know the type. It's right on top of a hill from the highway, lit up neon like a beacon for the guy to see when he drives home. For a while, he can just ignore it. But then one day as he's driving home from work, he says it's like he got possessed or something. All of a sudden, his car is veering toward the exit. Then, next thing you know, he's ordering a shot and a beer at the bar. Then he's on a two-week-long bender, and he's right back where he started."

I was listening to his story, but I continued to tell myself that I would be different. Given a challenge, I could survive anything.

"Moral is: even if you're mentally one hundred percent sure that you won't touch it, once you get put back into the environment that made you drink, that conditioning kicks in. If you go back home, or even near home, you're going to be putting yourself back into that environment, and even worse, now you're going to be alone there. You can jack off three times a day for a while, but, I mean, eventually it's going to be too much."

I humored him. "Fine, fine, okay, I get it. Maybe I'll get an apartment in Corte Madera, then. But there's no way I'm moving into a sober living home. It would be embarrassing. I don't think I could tell anyone about where I was."

"You need to have a support system in place to keep you accountable."

I huffed and held my ground, literally crossing my arms like a petulant child.

He sighed. "At least take a day trip to see some of the sober living houses around here. We could arrange to have you take some tours tomorrow, and you can decide then."

"No no no," I instinctively said, but then I thought about it for a second and remembered I would do literally *anything* to leave the grounds of the rehab center for a bit. Maybe that was part of his plan all along. So, I agreed to go, confident that I wouldn't fall for whatever spiel they gave me to move into sober living.

The next day, I waited outside the facility like a kid going on a field trip. I imagined getting picked up by a double-decker bus with a guide saying through a speaker system, "Aaand on your left, you'll notice some alcoholics getting their lives together..."

Instead, a black sedan with tinted windows pulled up. The window slid down, and the driver, a large man with a black ponytail, reached into his back pocket and unfolded a piece of paper. He stared at it for several seconds before turning to me.

"Melen?" he asked.

"That's me."

He nodded his head for me to get in.

A couple bags of old McDonald's sat in the middle of my floor space, and he made no effort to move them. I kicked them aside and sat down. The car reeked of cigarettes. An ashtray sat in one of the cup holders.

"I'm Gary. You smoke?"

"Yeah, sure."

He pushed a cigarette halfway out of a quarter-full pack. I lit it, then rolled down the window and inhaled hard.

"So, do you, like, work for the rehab center?" I asked him.

"Nah, man. They just call me when they need someone to be driven around. Pretty easy job."

We both quietly smoked a few cigarettes on the way to our tour of the sober living complexes that line the North Bay.

The first and the second places were basically the same. The buildings sat in the middle of nondescript neighborhoods with tickytack condos. The homes looked like they hadn't seen a remodel in a few decades, and the people living in them were uniformly old men with droopy faces. They had an air of total resignation, reinforcing everything I already thought.

Still, I was enjoying the freedom of being out on the road with Gary, who spent three-quarters of the drive selecting music on his phone — an alternation of reggae and death metal.

Finally, we pulled up to the third facility in San Rafael. The complex, which was really just a couple of small apartment buildings in close proximity, sat right on the water. It had a modern-looking front entrance that almost seemed like I could convince people was just an apartment. Maybe I could just say I was downsizing!

"This place isn't bad."

"Yeah, this one's legit," said Gary, inhaling his cigarette.

I met the house supervisor, Dominic, a huge guy with tattoos all over his body. He shook my hand. His palm was huge and calloused.

"We keep things strict, but we're fair," he said. "We've got a good community here. Let me see if any of the other guys are around."

He went and knocked on one of the doors, then came back with a man who looked about a decade younger than me. His name was Chase.

We quickly found out we had a lot in common. Chase told me he had a one-year-old baby who he was trying to win back, and he said coming here had helped convince the baby's mother that he was committed to change.

"Moving here was the best choice I could've made," he said. "I didn't want to do it at first, either, but it's the only way I'm going to get closer to my daughter. You should think about it, too."

I expressed my reservations, but when we ended the conversation, I said, "Hell, maybe I'll see you again soon."

I got back into Gary's car thinking about what Chase said. It felt like this was somewhere I could actually live, not just exist in a kind of suspension until something better came along. So, when I got back to rehab, I went to Dan and conceded. I'd stay at sober living.

"You're making the right choice—for yourself and your family," he said, and I could see the relief on his face.

But I puffed my chest one more time and made one demand, like a death row prisoner's last meal. I wanted to spend just one night at my house in Tiburon before going to sober living. I wanted to prove to myself and to Dan that I could handle it.

"You really like to turn everything into a competition, don't you?"

"What can I say? It keeps me going."

He considered for a second, then shrugged as if to say, *It's not the best idea, but do whatever you've gotta do.* I felt good about my decision, and when I went back to my room, I grabbed my phone out of a pair of socks and texted Jennifer what I was doing.

*You can't come home,* she replied.

*What do you mean? It's my house.*
*I'm coming back for just one night.*
*I want to see Mia.*

*If you're coming, then Mia and I are leaving.*
*What? No. You can't do that.*
*You signed over custody.*

I cursed, knowing there was nothing I could do. It finally became tangible just what I had given up by signing that paperwork.

\* \* \*

The last week in rehab couldn't have gone any slower. My friends and roommates, Andy and Chad, had both already finished their thirty days and gotten out. My new roommate was a meth-head who had a habit of pacing around the room and scratching his body. Meth-mites.

And the characters who came into rehab became more and more ... interesting. A middle aged man with a huge tattoo on his forearm that said *FREEDOM* in bold red letters came during my third week. We chatted over a cigarette one day, and he told me the story. He had apparently locked himself in his closet for two weeks doing crystal meth. He was totally psychotic and delusional.

One of his friends, who was a Satanist and a tattoo artist, made him some kind of deal to get out of the closet. He never said the deal, but I'm sure it had something to do with the devil. When he came out, he poured the rest of his meth into some tattoo ink and used it to tattoo the word on his arm. Then he came straight to rehab.

*Jesus Christ.* "Did... did that get you high?"

He looked at me like I was insane and didn't say anything.

I was ready to hop the fence and bolt out of there, but I reminded myself of what happened the first time I left rehab early. So, for the last week I put my head down and went to meeting after meeting until all the lessons, higher-power-surrendering and stories became a jumbled mush in my head.

Finally, my release date came. I didn't want to ask anyone, Jen included, for any favors to give me a ride home. Instead, I got creative and called a limo driver named Bijan who I had used for big events in San Francisco over the past twenty years. He was cheaper than a taxi. No one had seen somebody leave rehab in a limo, I'm sure. I left late that afternoon in absolute style, poking my head out of the sunroof and yelling, "So long, and good luck!"

\* \* \*

I already knew that when I took my first step back inside my house, it wasn't going to be the same. I wouldn't be greeted with the pitter-patter of Mia's feet and her voice shouting, "Daddy!" Jennifer wouldn't speak-shout a "Hi" from her office. But even knowing this, I had to give myself a pep talk when we pulled up to the house, and my body went a little numb when I opened the door and was greeted with silence.

Nothing inside my house was physically different. The family photos, taken at the beach when Mia was two years old, lined the walls in the entryway. The hardwood floor still just barely creaked as the shine of the recent home remodel wore into a dull earthy tone. The decorations and the rustic cabinets—the products of hours of consultations with interior design pros—still announced their costly presence. But without the people who filled it, the house felt completely foreign, like stepping into a childhood home as an adult, only to find the new homeowner painted over your dinosaur wallpaper.

I tried to push down those feelings, knowing I had precious few hours before I'd be back to living under rules and having roommates. I had to live it up as much as I could in the meantime. I took my pants off and turned on the TV, then sprawled out on the couch, starfish style.

It took less than an hour for me to become bored out of my mind, and I couldn't sleep, so I started wandering aimlessly through the house. My feet carried me down the stairs. I saw the arched door of the wine cellar and walked toward it. The door always hummed and slightly vibrated from the twenty-four-hour generator inside. Over several years, I had filled it with whatever rare and expensive bottles I came across. For every house-guest, the first interesting talking point came when I said, "Come check out the cellar." It helped validate that I didn't have a problem — I was just a collector.

Now, I stood outside the door to the cellar and thought of how central this place had been to my spiral. Before, my friends and I would spend hours in there, losing track of how many glasses, then how many bottles, we'd drank while we reminisced on the good days.

I thought of what Dan had said in rehab. I didn't want to be the guy who veers off the highway to the sports bar and then throws everything in the trash. But I also didn't want to shield my eyes as I passed it on the highway. I wanted to be the guy who could be around this, who could still control himself even if alcohol was present. I didn't want to be powerless, I wanted to be powerful. I needed the challenge.

I put my hand on the cold metal door, a small part of me wondering if I was going to fail. If this would just bring me back to where I was before rehab. I tried to turn the handle just a little bit, but it stuck with a click.

Locked. It was never locked. I wasn't even sure where the key would be.

I stood there for a minute, listening to the generator humming inside of the cellar, my hand still on the doorknob.

So that was it. Jennifer's distrust for me at this point was so high that she locked up the wine cellar and took away the key. She wasn't going to let me fuck up again, and she thought that given the temptation, I would. I felt angry for a second, and then sad.

I turned around and walked back up from the wine cellar and through this house that used to be home. I'd spent two years remodeling this bastard, going over endless paint wheels and tile schemes, deciding whether we wanted a double sink or a single, an island counter or not, a sectional couch or a three-seater, all to create the perfect place that could surround a happy family. Every room was painted a different color—our house was painted seven different god damn colors! Two years later, and what had been the point? Where was the happiness? Could I find it in the new hardwood floors? Was it hiding in the state-of-the-art garbage disposal? I had spent all this money filling this space with all sorts of stuff, and it was totally empty.

I walked back out onto my deck as the early hours of the morning crept on. The hillside was overwhelmingly quiet. I stood against the railing for a long time, frozen in uncertainty, waiting for divine intervention to tell me what I needed to do. It was strange being out there without a glass of wine. The wine always made me numb, kept my mind from racing all over the place.

I was startled out of a trance when a few high voices started to break the night's silence. Those damn birds, chirping in the brush below. They were joined by others until the noise became a city unto itself, one just waking up for the new day. The noise made me recoil, like Pavlov's dog in reverse.

But this time, as those birds cawed out dawn, I thought, *I don't have to be like this.* I'm not a brooder, lurking around a house alone without anything to do, trapped in my thoughts. I'm a person who goes and does things. Gets shit done. Those birds did their same damn thing every morning, pissing me off to no end. Why couldn't I be like them?

I went back inside and opened one of the cabinets in my bedroom. I pulled out the box marked STEVE MEMORIES and laid it on my bed.

On top were all the photos of me and my adoptive parents. In one photo, my mom and dad stood with their hands on my shoulders while I wore a too-big baseball cap and held a trophy. I was about ten years old in the photo, with bleach-blond hair and a big smile across my face.

Further down in the mix were receipts from movies and first dates, old fliers for my high school baseball team, and some of my better-scoring essays from school.

I set that pile to the side. Then I saw it. Somehow, when I saw the red fire truck, I knew it was what I was looking for the whole time. I felt a wave of emotions run through me as I remembered. *You're safe.* The truck's paint was worn to a dull orange. I turned the rubber wheels with my finger, and they clicked with dust.

This was the one thing that made a one-year-old boy feel safe, that made him feel comfortable and happy and loved in the face of true abandonment. It was the one thing that made me feel like I belonged somewhere, and no matter what I did, I wasn't going to be alone.

I sat on my bed holding the fire truck for a long time as the rising sun brightened my room. Once again, I couldn't imagine how I could get any lower. Losing my family felt worse, in a way, than any of the cancer pain ever did. But this time felt like there was really *nothing,* that I was at ground zero, and I had still survived.

I spun the rubber wheels and wondered what could take the place of this fire truck for my adult self. What could tell me that I was going to get through this all, that I had the power to keep moving forward? Then I thought of Mia, of how imagining her without a father had propelled me through chemotherapy and radiation. She had kept me from giving up, whether she knew it or not. Maybe there wasn't anything like this fire truck for me, now. But maybe I could be that for Mia again. She could see me and know: *I'm safe.*

I had nothing, and it felt like I had everything to win back.

# CHAPTER
# SEVENTEEN

 "Goddammit," I said, simultaneously trying to move the cup and adjust my aim until they matched. Instead, I went from pissing on my hand to pissing on the floor.

A knock on the door. "Everything okay in there?" It was Dominic, the manager of the sober living complex, from just outside. He startled me, even though I knew he was there.

"Yeah, yeah, all good."

I hit the sweet spot—stream straight into cup.

He sighed, loudly conveying his displeasure that this was part of the job description. "Hurry up in there, alright? I'm not paid by the hour."

I grabbed some paper towels and stomped on the wet floor, then washed the warm bottle in the sink. I wondered for a moment how long it had been since I smoked pot and then remembered, *You were just in rehab, smart guy.*

I washed my hands and opened the door, offering the pee to Dominic with a shit-eating grin. "Microwaved it for you," I said.

His heavily tattooed arms crossed, he huffed and made an intentionally slow motion to take the cup from me. I knew I was pushing my limits a bit with him, but I thought he'd respond to a little prodding. He had spent time in Pelican Bay, the prison for people who are too dangerous even for San Quentin. I wanted to laugh that this guy who had probably been a don in a California prison system gang was now holding my warm piss.

"Need to hydrate, bro," he said.

I laughed. "I'll work on that."

"You're a funny guy. Come with me."

He took me through the complex, which had four bedrooms shared between seven men, a kitchen and a living room with mismatched furniture all surrounding a TV.

On the far side of the living room stood a whiteboard with each house member's name along the top of a column. Below each person's name were words like *DISHES* or *BATHROOM* or *VACUUM*—chores for the week. The next line shouted *SPONSOR* and was filled with names and phone numbers ... except for my blank column. And last, announcing its presence in bright red, was a line for *SOBER SINCE*. For the people who had been sober the longest, that row was marked just with a year—2008, 2010. The intermediate range of residents had a month and a year. And then there was mine, marked with a month, a day, and a year—May 2, 2013. The freshman class, still counting in individual days.

It was intimidating. I felt like I was joining the PGA Tour of sobriety, and I'd be shanking all my shots into the rough while these gloved pros stood with their hands on their hips, waiting for me to play.

"We have a lot of rules here, but we're fair," Dominic said. "No drugs, no alcohol, obviously. Weekly urine tests. Ninety meetings in ninety days. Do your chores. No guests. Follow those rules, and you can stay here as long as you want."

I wanted to ask: *What's the shortest period of time I can stay here and get what I need to get out of it?* Instead, I asked, "How long do people usually stay here?"

"Some of the ones who do the best have been here for years. Others... for less time. Take Bob over here, I'll introduce you."

He brought me to one of the rooms and knocked on the door.

Out walked a sleepy-eyed older man in a Led Zeppelin t-shirt. Dominic spoke, "Bob's been here longer than I have. He's, what, ten years without a drink?"

"Ten years," Bob repeated.

"That's impressive," I said. "Congrats. What do you do for a living?"

"I work at the Lucky's grocery store across the freeway."

Bob didn't exactly scream success to me. In fact, a lot of the guys here seemed a little checked out from life. Another guy worked in insurance sales and had kids who wanted nothing to do with him. And there was yet another person who worked at a Lucky's grocery store.

I immediately started sizing myself up next to them. Maybe this place would really help me stay sober by the sheer pressure of seeing these people who had done it so long.

Dominic then walked me to my room, at the back of the complex, with a door leading to the back deck where you could see sailboats floating through the San Rafael canals. My bed, right behind the door, was a twin, like I was back in my freshman year of college. I really was taking a step back here from how far I had gotten in life.

I met my two roommates. On the far side of the room, his bed somewhat separated by a hospital-sheet partition, was Mike, a hardened guy in his fifties who was the other guy working at Lucky's. He was an ex-marine who smoked four packs of unfiltered Camels a day and had a somber, quiet demeanor. Watching him made me feel better about my burgeoning smoking habit. I gave him his space, and we got along fine.

The other roommate was Chase, the young surfer guy who I had met on the tour of this place back when I was in rehab. Always walking with his chest puffed out, he seemed like one of those guys who gets into fights over surf spots. But like me, he was trying to get clean for his daughter, so we bonded quickly.

"How long are you thinking about staying here?" Chase asked when Dominic excused himself.

"Honestly, I don't want to spend too much time here. I want to get an apartment so I can have my daughter sleep over. But I have to be here to regain trust, to get a better custody arrangement."

"I feel you on that. It's been months already, and I'm pretty ready to get out of here myself."

"Yeah. For now, I just have to get visitation rights back. I'm dreading my first supervised visit. I'm gonna be supervised by my ex or her mom. Can you imagine?"

He shook his head. "Every step is a step, though." He paused. "By the way, you might want to get some earplugs. The, uh, crickets are pretty loud out here at night."

"Good to know, thanks."

That night, I went with Chase and a couple of the other younger guys to get In-n-Out. After an hour on the toilet, with my intestines screaming at me that we really needed a stomach to deal with this, I got in bed early for work the next day. I said goodnight to my two new roommates and fell quickly into a dreamless sleep ...

... Until I woke up to the sound of someone taking a quick, hard breath, like sipping out of an empty cup through a straw. I sat up and looked around. It was still pitch black. I checked the clock—3 a.m. The voice started panting furiously, until it turned into a *SLUUUUURP* and finally exploded.

*Ah—ahh—AHHH! AHHHHHH! AHHHHHHHHHHHH!*

"What the fuck?" I said as I jumped out of bed. I ran over to the door and flipped on the light. The sheet covering Mike's bed was vibrating like a gale of wind was behind it.

*Ahhhh!* It continued, a primal scream that made me think Mike was getting stabbed and soon I'd see splatters of blood darken the sheet.

Chase finally rolled over in his bed and opened his eyes. He pulled something out of his ears, but he didn't get up as the screaming continued.

"What the fuck?" I said in his direction.

"That's just Mike," he said calmly. "He does that."

"Jesus Christ! What do you mean?"

Chase didn't say anything, and finally, the screaming stopped, just as suddenly as it started. The canal crickets took over, and I could feel my heartbeat in my skull.

Mike's voice, shockingly lucid, came from behind the sheet. "Who turned the fucking light on?"

"Me! You were screaming!"

"Well, shut it off."

I stood there trying to catch my breath and struggling to think of something to say. But given that he casually addressed me as if *I* was the one bothering *him,* I shut off the light and got back in bed. I lay there awake for hours, thinking of how assured I would be that no one would be screaming in the middle of the night if I was home.

That morning, Chase eyed me with a smile in the kitchen.

"Told you those crickets were loud."

"Jesus. You weren't kidding." I lowered my voice. "What's wrong with him?"

Chase told me what he had heard from other roommates, that when Mike was a kid, his mother had been shot in the face right in front of him, and he relived it over and over in his dreams.

"I can't really get mad at the guy, then," I said.

I started sleeping with earplugs, and his blood-curdling screams only incorporated themselves into my dreams.

* * *

Things were quiet, figuratively speaking, for the next few days. I had fully recommitted myself to being a good employee, since that was the main facet of my life I could impact for the time being. I was back to waking up before the sun rose and hitting the stock market right when it opened for the day.

On the morning of my fourth day, I rolled out of bed and put on my pajama bottoms. I could hear Mike still snoring from the other bed, but Chase's was unmade and empty. Odd, I thought, he didn't seem like the type to rise early.

The kitchen was still dark, and I left the light off to give my eyes a minute to adjust. I reached up to my cabinet and pulled out a coffee filter and some grounds, then put them into the shitty drip machine and turned it on. All these years after cancer, I still woke up with a ghost pain where my stomach was. Coffee seemed to be the only thing that could help it, or maybe my body had just convinced itself of that.

I turned and put a piece of bread in the toaster while the coffee brewed. But something caught the corner of my eye. The sofa. There, lying with the upper part of his torso on the cushion and his lower half slumped on the floor, was Chase. His head was sideways, foam rolling out of his mouth and dripping onto his shoulder.

"Shit, shit, FUCK," I said. I walked over to him, expecting him to already be dead. But his eyes were slightly open, and he was still breathing—gasping, really—his breath coming in a horrific, metallic *heeeeuuu, heeuuuu,* as foam continued to stream out of his mouth like an overflowing dishwasher. I ran out to Dominic's room, banged on the door and blurted broken sentences to the sleepy-eyed man who emerged.

"OD! I think, OD! In the living room!" I thought ridiculously for a second that I really needed a cup of coffee to deal with this.

Dominic rushed over and assessed the situation with the quiet confidence of someone who's seen this before. He calmly called 911.

After a few minutes watching my unresponsive roommate, I heard a siren outside. Four paramedics strolled in, talking to each other like they'd just walked in the front door of a diner for breakfast. They stood in a semicircle around the sofa and soaked in the situation.

One of the paramedics came up to me. "You the first one who saw him?"

"Yeah. I'm his roommate."

"Has he taken anything recently that you know of?"

"Not that I know of, but this is a sober living home." I wanted to ask why the hell they were asking me questions and not doing anything about the man heaving on the sofa.

The paramedic asked me more questions about Chase: his name, his weight, how long ago I saw him. I really thought we were reaching a turning point, and these guys were just going to let him die while they stood over him, until finally one of the paramedics turned to the radio on his shoulder.

"Unit 51 on scene. Likely overdose. Responding."

Then, as slow as everything had gone before that, everything after happened in a flash. The radio paramedic nodded to a burly guy who was closest to Chase. The man reached into his chest pocket and pulled out a small white packet. He bit the packaging and ripped the top off, spat it out, and grabbed a small needle from inside. Without hesitating, he jabbed the needle into Chase.

Suddenly, Chase's eyes looked like they were about to explode. *HEEEEUUUUUUHHHHHHHH.*

Rarely do movies look so close to real life, but my god did he jump up just like Uma Thurman in Pulp Fiction.

Then, unlike Mrs. Wallace, he fell back down just as quickly as he rose, his head whipping back against the couch cushion. His breathing came in short bursts.

And just like that, it was over.

"Uh, is he good?" I asked.

"He'll be okay," the burly paramedic said, putting a respirator over Chase's face.

They brought in a stretcher and took him away, talking about what they were going to get for breakfast when their shift ended. Meanwhile my toast sat burnt in the toaster, and I stood there with my mouth open.

"Well, fuck," I said to Dominic. "That was gnarly."

"I can't believe he fucking did that. Glad you saw him though. Good job."

Chase stayed in the ER for three days. On the second day, I had the chance to go visit him and get his story. Apparently, his girlfriend had showed up outside the sober living home with heroin and a vague proposal of sex. He went outside to meet her, then muscle memory kicked in: wrap the rubber band around the arm, measure out the dosage, and shoot up into the cleanest vein. But of course, he'd been sober for a couple months, so doing his usual amount was a shock to the system.

"Why'd you do it, though?"

He looked away from me. "When I see it, when it's there, I just ... my mind shuts down. I just did it."

"I really thought you guys were all pros. I thought I was the only one worried about fucking up."

"We're all on the knife's edge, man."

Things felt different at sober living after Chase's OD. It was like a veil had been lifted from my eyes, and I now saw this place for what it was. It wasn't the safehouse where people would behave correctly because everyone else would hold each other accountable. In reality, everyone here was standing over a cliff, some of them just one step away from taking that drink, from falling back into the pit.

* * *

My first supervised visit with Mia came just over a week into my time in sober living. Jen and I were communicating mostly by terse email, with each of Jen's emails signed with the impersonal: "Regards, Jennifer." I had no leverage in the situation, so I had to agree to her demands that every visit be supervised by either Jen's mother or, if she wasn't available, by Fabiana, at our house in Tiburon.

Jen had already left the house by the time I pulled into our driveway. I hadn't seen Mia in more than a month, and I couldn't escape the feelings of guilt over how much time I just hadn't been with her.

But all that evaporated when she rushed out the door, yelling, "Daddy!" I crouched down and she lunged into my arms. I squeezed her tight and lifted her into the air.

"I missed you so much!" she said.

"I missed you too, sweet girl."

I saw Jen's mom, Linda, leaning against the door.

"Hi," I said to her.

"Hi, Steve. It's good to see you."

We walked inside, Mia now on my back like a monkey.

"I'll make you some food and give you all some time to catch up," Linda said.

I sat with Mia on the sofa. "Tell me all about your summer. I hear you learned how to ride your bike without training wheels."

"Yeah! I can ride all the way down the driveway."

"I'm so proud of you."

She looked down, something clearly on her mind.

"What's up, Mia? Tell me what you're thinking."

"Why can't you stay here with us, daddy?"

I felt tears coming into my eyes but held them back. "I'm sorry, baby. Your mom and I just can't live together right now. But that doesn't mean we don't love you. I want to see you as much as I can. We're going to have as much fun time together as we ever have."

"Okay, just don't leave again, alright?"

"I won't. I promise, I won't."

During my stay, Mia and I ate dinner and watched movies. Linda mostly stayed out of our way, but I still felt like a prisoner being let out in the yard, given a semblance of freedom without being able to hop over the fence.

Still, I felt that I was on the right path. I knew from earlier in life when my parents died that all pain can heal if given the space for that healing. If I fixed the things that caused Jen to lose her trust in me — my drug and alcohol abuse — she wouldn't want to keep this custody arrangement forever. Then, we could heal. I could get my time with Mia back. I just needed to be perfect.

# CHAPTER
# EIGHTEEN

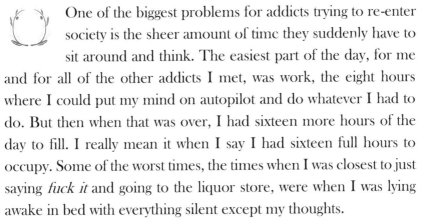 One of the biggest problems for addicts trying to re-enter society is the sheer amount of time they suddenly have to sit around and think. The easiest part of the day, for me and for all of the other addicts I met, was work, the eight hours where I could put my mind on autopilot and do whatever I had to do. But then when that was over, I had sixteen more hours of the day to fill. I really mean it when I say I had sixteen full hours to occupy. Some of the worst times, the times when I was closest to just saying *fuck it* and going to the liquor store, were when I was lying awake in bed with everything silent except my thoughts.

People know this, and for that reason, one of the requirements of staying at the sober living home was to attend ninety Alcoholics Anonymous meetings in the first ninety days. Supposedly, it takes ninety days to turn a new action into a habit. I had to turn sobriety into an activity— rather than just *not* drinking, I had to turn it into something productive that I could go and do.

I started by getting my AA meetings done in the morning before work. The crowd at those meetings skewed largely toward my own demographic—people in business attire, many checking their watches and keeping their heads down with the distractedness of a full day's work ahead.

Going to those meetings checked the boxes, but I quickly found it wasn't enough. When I got home from work, I'd go to the house and sit around on the couch in the living room. While I was watching TV surrounded by claustrophobic, asylum-ward-white walls, anxiety crept up on me, and thoughts of *What the fuck am I doing?* and *How did I get here?* took over my head. Then the thought would come back of how great a glass of wine would be to take the edge off the day.

So I started going to more meetings. The after-work crowd was, for whatever reason, more depressing than the before-work crowd. They were older, red- and droopy-eyed. But I found that going to meetings before and after work was great for surrounding my day, giving me a sort of cocoon of support.

But society doesn't make it easy to be sober. One day, I had planned a lunch meeting with a big-time new client. I was really nervous for the meeting, because it would make a difference of thirty percent to my income for the year. In the morning, I ran over the lunch meeting in my head a million times, and I thought it wouldn't be a bad idea to get a beer. For one, I didn't want him to think I was weird or feel bad if he ordered alcohol. Besides that, it would help calm me down. The thoughts started to cascade on themselves, until I started to think I really had *no choice* but to get a beer at lunch. But I took a step back and was able to recognize exactly what was happening in my head. I decided to go to an AA meeting before the lunch.

When I got there, I was in a bad mood, sitting in the back of the room with a shitty little styrofoam coffee while the room sat half-empty. How was I doing both this and going to a country club for lunch to discuss six-figure investments? The contrast was just too stark.

During the AA meeting, a young, skinny woman approached the microphone, her high heels clacking on the tile floor of the community center. She was dressed like an executive, wearing a pencil skirt and a black blazer, her hair a shiny straightened blond.

She started her story with confidence, but her voice wavered as she went on.

"I started drinking when I was young. Thirteen. My mom had died, and I had just moved to a new town to live with my grandparents. Drinking helped me feel like I belonged, like I could fit in with all these kids who already knew each other. I blacked out a few times, but not that much. It was all just fun."

The story continued the way so many do—one of her parents died, and suddenly the drinking took a turn. Now, it wasn't about having fun anymore. It was numbing the pain, coping with what had happened. Then she was blacking out a couple of nights a week, and then she was drinking alone, and then she was driving drunk, and then she got in a car wreck.

Her story hit me like a brick, because while it was unique in some of the details, it was a total formula. It was *my* formula. The drinking started as just a fun thing to do, and then something happened that caused it to take a turn. And then the thought was: *If only I hadn't gotten cancer, I wouldn't have spiraled down and down like this. If only P.J. had survived, if only my wife hadn't divorced me. If if if...*

But right then it dawned on me that the thing about drinking is it always tricks us into believing something external caused life to turn to shit. It was *just this one thing* that caused the spiral down into oblivion, and it wouldn't be the same this time if I had another drink—I'd be aware of what it was that brought me down and wouldn't let it happen again.

But it never is just one thing. It wasn't just the cancer that caused my drinking to turn from a fun time to a coping mechanism. During all those drunken nights before it got so serious, alcohol was slowly wrapping itself around me. At first it felt comforting, like a blanket, like something warm embracing me and keeping me safe — safe from judgement, from embarrassment, from whatever. But then it started to seem less like a blanket and more like some creature's tentacles wrapping me up loosely. I let it happen, though, because alcohol had been good to me in the past, leading me to some of the best nights of my life. Then, once the opportunity came—when I got cancer, when P.J. Gallaway died—suddenly all those tentacles already around my body tightened, and *now* I understood I had been in danger the whole time. Then they pulled me down below the floorboards into darkness.

"Anyway," she continued, pulling me out of my thoughts. "Maybe I'm just on the pink cloud, but I'm really excited every morning when I wake up now. I want to embrace this next chapter."

She left the stage, and everybody applauded. When the meeting ended, I leaned forward to a guy sitting ahead of me. He was around my age, with a nerdy look and some thin glasses low on his nose.

"Hi, do you mind if I ask. What did she mean by 'pink cloud?'"

"Oh, that's what you call it when you feel really good after getting sober. Like when you see a really nice sunset, and everything about your life is so clear and exciting. You realize you could've been dead in a ditch with a needle in your arm, but instead you're here and alive, and drinking was stupid anyway."

"Sounds like a good place to be."

"Well, it's the time when you have to be the most careful. Because when those plans don't go exactly how you want them, you fall back into old habits. My name is Ron, by the way."

"Nice to meet you. I'm Steve."

I realized soon after that meeting that I was definitely on the pink cloud. I was diving headfirst into sobriety, telling all of my friends about it, and rejoicing in the fact that it felt like I had an extra day of my life every week without experiencing any hangovers.

Tanya and I even arranged our first date, at the Del Mar races in July. I had to get special permission from Dominic to go. He chided me that it wasn't a good idea, but I promised him I was ready for it, and he relented.

It was nerve-racking, not only because it was my first real sober outing. We had only been communicating by text up until that point, and I could convey a lot of confidence in that medium. In person, while sober, I didn't think I could be as sure of myself. I was still only 130 pounds. My elbows were still thicker than my biceps. Would she think I was a man?

When she picked me up, though, I knew we had something going for us beyond an internet relationship. We went to the racetrack. Everyone there was drinking or already drunk. We sat down in the box seats and I told Tanya she should have a glass of champagne.

"Are you sure? I don't want you to feel bad."

"I'll be fine. I'm good."

"You're stronger than most people I know."

I wanted to kiss her, but it was harder to make the move without any booze in me. I had to create the confidence that I never thought I had without liquid courage. But, hell, I was on the pink cloud. I could create anything I wanted, especially when I was with her.

I leaned over and kissed her for the first time in twenty-five years. It was unlike anything I had felt in years. If this was what the pink cloud felt like, I didn't ever want to leave.

* * *

I was in the pink cloud at the same time as a lot of my friends from AA and rehab, and the way we all seemed to keep alcohol at bay was by keeping our hands busy and staying out of our heads.

A few weeks after my date with Tanya, I went with Chad and Andy, my two roommates from rehab, along with my new sober living roommate Danny, to my house in Lake Tahoe for the weekend.

The house was huge, with eight bedrooms, a massive twenty-foot bar, and a big game room. It was strange driving up there without Jen or Mia. The guys marveled at the bar, and Andy pretended to pour shots. The liquor cabinet was still filled with very real alcohol.

We went on a hike in Squaw Valley the first day. It was late summer, and a pine smell hung in the hot mountain air. At one point, Andy and I broke off from Danny and Chad and hiked up to the top of a rock that overlooked the whole valley.

It was one of those places that lends itself to deep, philosophical thought, and that was where our conversation headed.

"I've been talking to a shaman," Andy said. "I want to try *ayahuasca*. I think it might really put everything into a bigger perspective and get my music career going again."

I looked at him skeptically. "You want to do a drug to fix your drug problem?"

He laughed. "It's different from that, man. This stuff gives totally revolutionary thought. It's not a substance you'd want to abuse. It's something to open your mind."

"Well, okay, then," I said, already worried about him.

"And you know, I think I can probably drink again," he said. "Not like, now, obviously, but at some point in the future. I think I'll be able to do it."

I gave him a look, then turned away to gaze at the beautiful valley below us. We were so high above everything else. How likely was it that we would fall? We sat there for a long time, silent. "Let's head back down," I said.

We marched down the hill and found the slackers, Chad and Danny, sitting on a rock near the base of the mountain. Then we all hiked back to the cabin and decided we should go to an AA meeting before dinner.

We found a session in a building right on the lake. It was a beautiful backdrop that made me feel like I was really doing something proactive by going to these AA meetings. I wasn't just focusing on the absence of activity—not drinking.

Dinner was different. We went to a steakhouse just nearby and sat around the booth as the waiter handed us menus and tried to pass a huge wine list. Danny waved it away and said, "Four waters, please."

The waiter lingered with the drink menu outstretched for a little too long, looking offended. I felt like explaining that we were just sober, not cheap, but he pulled it away and walked over to get our waters.

"I like being sober and all, but there's really nothing like a glass of red wine with a steak," I said.

"No joke," Chad said. "Last time I was at a steakhouse with my wife, we got a hundred-dollar bottle. Best wine I've had in my life."

"Last time I was in a booth like this," Danny said, already cracking himself up, "I drank so much that I went under the table and yakked on my girlfriend's feet."

"Jesus!" I said. "How did that go over?"

"Oh, I mean, she left me like a couple weeks later."

"Christ," Andy said. "What a downer. Melen, tell one of your cancer stories to bring the mood up."

After we ate and the bill was paid, Chad suggested we try hitting one of the bars to see what it was like just to do that while sober.

There was a second of silence at the table, before Danny chimed in, "Hell, yeah. Let's do it."

Andy shrugged.

I was hesitant at first, but then I did a few mental backflips. "Maybe it wouldn't be the worst thing. We could be there to support each other. Exposure therapy!"

We went to Pete and Peter's, a dive bar in Tahoe City that I used to come to and get drunk during winter trips.

It was about 8 p.m., earlier in the evening than I had ever been there. A few older people sat on barstools taking slow sips out of pint glasses, but other than that, it was empty. I felt tired already.

I ordered a non-alcoholic beer, thinking maybe that could trick my brain into having fun. The other guys got Red Bulls. We sat around a booth and suddenly confronted the problem of not knowing what the fuck to do or talk about. Andy looked antsy, rapping his knuckles on the wood and looking around him to see if the scenery would change from one second to the next.

"Pool?" Danny suggested.

Chad nodded overeagerly. We got up and over the next hour shot twenty bucks' worth of barroom pool.

People started to arrive to the bar at a progressing level of drunkenness. It culminated when a gaggle of wasted bachelorette party girls, all wearing matching sashes, stumbled in the door and parked next to the pool tables, blocking us from playing. All four of us looked at each other for direction.

"Should we ask them to move?" Danny said to me.

"I don't think so."

Suddenly, the place was totally full, and the only four sober people inside were all standing huddled together like a football team.

The bachelorette party was taking shots loudly next to us, seemingly oblivious to our existence.

"Hey," I said to one of the presumable bridesmaids. "How long 'til the wedding?"

"A month," she said, her eyes half-closed.

I realized I didn't even really care to follow up—I could ask where it was, how she was related to the bride—but I just couldn't make myself get into it. I slunk away back to my friends, and they snickered at me.

Something started to tug at my mind. I had become the boring guy who was trying to play by all the rules to get my daughter back. But couldn't I just also have one night where I was the wild, fun Steve again? *Maybe I can have it all.*

I thought, maybe it would be okay if I ordered just one beer. I was with safe people who knew what I was going through, who wouldn't let me drag myself down. Maybe they'd pin me to the ground to force me to stop if I ordered more. Or maybe they'd slip a note to the bartender not to put any alcohol in my gin and tonic.

But then I remembered. *It's not like I'm with the Green Berets of sobriety. These guys and I are like the Cub Scouts. Shit, any one of us is probably just waiting for someone else to make the first move toward the bar.*

Suddenly, I realized I only had two choices. Either I was going to stay here, and sooner or later I was going to drink, or I would leave. There would be no middle ground, no more dancing around it. That was it. And what would happen if I drank? I would set myself back in everything I was trying to work for.

"Guys, I have to go," I said.

They all looked at me for a second, and then Chad responded, "No problem, we're gone."

"Don't even worry about it, we can go," Danny said.

Andy nodded.

And just like that, we walked out the door, out of the thick and musky barroom air and into the crisp mountain wind. It was strangely quiet outside, the mountains lit up by a nearly full moon. It was beautiful, and I almost wanted to cry.

"Guys, I know I'm not very good at being serious, but I really appreciated that. That was one of the only times I've had a drink within reach and turned it down. And I knew I had to do it to get my daughter back, but it was you guys who enabled me to do it."

Andy hugged me. "And we know you'd do the same for us."

* * *

When I went to my first AA meeting back in the Bay Area and told everyone there about the trip, they said I was crazy. Why would I go back to my house that had a twenty-foot bar and a kegerator?

"Why would you put yourself back into a bar so soon?" the facilitator asked me. "You're just asking for a relapse."

"It might not make sense, but I think I have to do things like that. To really succeed, I need to be proving people wrong about me. Maybe I need to even prove myself wrong. I need the challenge."

They looked at me disapprovingly. But I thought I knew myself, and I continued doing things that garnered frowns from my fellows in sobriety.

A few months after our trip, Andy got kicked out of his own sober living home for staying out past curfew. He moved back in with his parents in Placerville, a suburban town in the foothills of the Sierras. His music career had basically stalled, and he developed all sorts of odd hobbies. He became particularly enamored with motorcycles.

For his twenty-seventh birthday, Andy invited Chad, Danny, me and a girl named Katie who had been with him in sober living to his family home for a day of sober debauchery. The checklist included skydiving, a gun range, and a casino.

First up was skydiving. As I sat in the airplane strapped to a man dressed like Batman, I thought of my life, of how I should have been dead already. How often was I going to experience something like this? I asked him to go as crazy as we could, and he bent the rules to spin me around and around a million times before switching to spiral the other way like a toilet in South America. When we hit the ground, I exclaimed to the other guys and Katie, "Holy shit, that was a better rush than drinking!"

We took our harnesses off and, like walking sacks of testosterone, headed straight to the gun range. I had brought my grandfather's shotgun, a huge wood rifle.

I lit a cigarette to keep the head high going and puffed in and out while holding the gun against my shoulder.

"Pull!"

The dish came flying horizontally. I tracked it for several seconds until it was at the top of its arc. Then, with a pull of the trigger, the gun kicked like a mule against my shoulder, while the skeet kept sailing on its way. Miss. A bad miss. I missed about five more before I actually hit one.

Andy wanted to take things to the next level, so he rented a mammoth M82 rifle. The bullets alone for that thing cost about ten bucks apiece. He asked if I wanted to shoot it, and I noted that the kickback from that might make me lose a couple more organs. I spotted for him, though, and when he shot at the target, the shock wave still knocked me on my ass.

"Damn," he said, clearly blown away, even though he missed the target by a mile. He shot five more bullets from that gun, and when he finally hit the target, it made a four-foot hole.

After the range, we had time to go back to his parents' place for dinner before our last stop on our night of sober debauchery: the casino.

At dinner, though, Andy was different. We were all tired, but he looked particularly heavy-eyed. He was talking just a little bit slower, and then sometimes speeding up his speech as if to compensate. He looked like someone on drugs who was trying to pull off not being on drugs.

His parents didn't seem to notice anything, and I was struck by the sad thought that they probably knew him better when he was high than when he was sober.

I pulled Danny aside right after dinner. "You notice Andy?"

"Yeah, totally," he said. "I saw some Percocet in his medicine cabinet. I think he's taking that."

We talked about whether or not to confront him about it, but we decided that since it was his birthday, we should hold off.

We drove to the Indian casino. I went to the blackjack table with fifty dollars, which I quickly lost, while the other guys played some of the cheaper tables. At 1 a.m., Andy, Katie and Chad said they wanted to go to a strip club to complete the night of decadence. Katie was now sitting on Andy's lap. It all just didn't seem that fun to me anymore. I didn't want to keep up this kind of lifestyle. I just wanted to be with my family.

"I don't have the energy to stay out this late anymore. Cancer sapped that out of me. I think I'm good."

Danny agreed and took a taxi with me back to the house. I hopped right in bed and fell asleep...

...Until I was awoken by a shaking sound that seemed like an earthquake, then took on a more definitive shape as a woman's voice. *What's she saying?* Oh, yep, definitely sex. I turned to the alarm clock, which said 3 a.m.

It got louder and louder, until the girl was screaming, piercing the otherwise silent night.

*Are you fucking kidding?* I thought. I couldn't believe Andy was doing this while his parents were sleeping upstairs. I put my head under my pillow and tried to fall back asleep.

The next morning, the unspoken agreement that *yeah, we all heard that last night* hung in the air. I felt like I couldn't look Andy's parents in the eyes.

Andy looked the same as he had the previous night—his eyes half-closed, his face just a little pale.

I pulled him outside. "What are you doing? What are you on?"

"What do you mean? Nothing, nothing, man. I'm just tired. I wouldn't do that."

"Don't fucking lie to me. I know when you're lying."

His head was lowered, his eyes on the ground. "I'm not. I promise."

"I can't hang out with you if you're on something. You know that."

He nodded and assured me one last time he wasn't on anything. I left it there, and we went back inside and finished breakfast.

As we said our goodbyes, though, I had to get one last word in.

"You know, I'm only asking because I really care about you. I just want to make sure you're okay."

"I know, I know. I appreciate it. But I'm good."

We clenched and patted each other on the back a few times, and then I turned around and left.

The next time I talked to him was on the phone several weeks later. He had been hanging out with Katie when she OD'd and had to be revived at the ER. He apologized to me. He didn't say why he was sorry, but I knew it was for lying. He never said what drugs he was on.

It was the last time I talked to him. A few months later, I got word that Andy had driven his motorcycle straight into a brick wall. He died on impact.

The toxicology report was never released publicly.

I was devastated by Andy's death. I blamed myself, and I wondered if there was something I should have done when I confronted him at his parents' house. Should I have hogtied him and dragged him to rehab? Or told his parents what was going on?

I didn't know, but the feeling that there was *something* I could have done burdened me.

After that, I resolved that I would never again be silent when someone clearly needed help. I would do whatever it took to help people get on the right path.

\* \* \*

But Andy's death also left me jaded with my living situation. The people in sober living didn't seem to be growing. They just seemed resigned to the place they were in, and they had no plans of ever leaving. I felt like I was seeing more failure than success.

For other people, surviving addiction might have been the hardest thing they've done. But for me, it wasn't. When I had cancer, I had a five percent chance I'd die on the operating table and an eighty-five percent chance I wouldn't make it out of the first couple of years. I faced death right before I underwent anesthesia. Then I went through chemotherapy and radiation, living another half-decade under the near-certainty that I was still probably going to die. Addiction was hard, but it wasn't as hard as that.

I knew that I had a lot to gain back, and I just couldn't do that here. Just a few months earlier, I had a wife and a daughter, and now I had neither. But I thought I'd be able to regain one of those two people if I got out of here and got my own apartment.

I could get back Mia—my inspiration.

# CHAPTER

# NINETEEN

Until I could get everything lined up to get my own place, my life was about doing the little things to regain trust.

While in sober living, I went to every single one of Mia's little league and soccer games. I came to parent-teacher conferences and was over-the-top nice to Jen, even when she would barely look at me. Other couples complimented us on how cordial we could be after our divorce, even if it was a curt cordiality.

By consistently showing up, day after day, as a new version of myself, I was able to convince Jen that this Steve was here to stay. Finally, I got an email from Jen that looked like it was written by a lawyer, proposing a probationary period where I would see Mia unsupervised for three days a week, two hours at a time from October until January. It wasn't what I wanted, but it was a start.

Then in December 2013, I told Dominic, the house manager, that after just five months at the sober living complex, I was ready to move out. It was basically a record for the complex—I was going to be one of the last ones to move in and the first to move out.

He looked like he was waiting for me to say I was joking. Then, when no joke materialized, he asked, "Where are you going?"

"I've got a two-bedroom apartment lined up back home in Tiburon." The second bedroom was so that Mia could sleep in the spare if needed.

"With any roommates?"

"No, it'll just be me."

He scoffed. "You aren't ready to be living alone yet. You're going to relapse for sure."

"I'll be fine. I'm just going to keep going to AA meetings and work to get my daughter back. I just feel like I've gotten everything I can get out of this place."

"You think that. But you're wrong."

I shrugged. "I've made it through worse."

Part of me thought he was jealous that I'd be able to move on with my life so quickly, while everyone else planted their roots in this little duplex.

But another part of me wondered if he might be right. Up until that point, I had spent my entire life living with other people: first with my parents, then with college roommates and friends, then with my wife and daughter, and finally with my sober living roommates. Since the beginning of my life, I always had people around me to communicate with whenever I needed to get out of my head. I had never been really alone, coming home every night to an empty, noiseless house. The thought did scare the shit out of me.

But I was determined—getting an apartment could be a solid display to Jen and her family that I had gotten my shit together. And it felt important to have a place where Mia could stay that was *our* new space, so I didn't have to do these embarrassing visits at my old home, where every new memory now belonged to Jen.

And Dominic's response was fuel to me. If there's anything I've always loved in life, it's proving people wrong. I had to prove I could still hold my job down after getting cancer, then I had to prove to Jen that I could go to rehab and finish it, even if it took me two tries.

Now, I had to prove to Dominic that I could stay sober without being in this home, and then I could give him a little *f- you* when I made it happen.

So that month I moved out of the sober living home and into my new apartment. Whereas I had started with one of the big ass houses near the top of the hill, not far from where people like Carlos Santana lived, now I was moving down the ridge into a complex with a bunch of wine-guzzling, small dog walking old ladies as neighbors.

The status that I had worked so hard for just evaporated. But that didn't matter, because the place I got was specifically for myself and Mia. I turned the spare room into a kid's room and set up a big play area in the living room.

Soon after I got the apartment, Jen granted my first sleepover with Mia. In the run-up to that evening, I was as excited as I had been for anything in my life.

When I was in rehab, it tortured me to think how much of that time with Mia I was missing out on. She was six years old, and she had grown tall and athletic for her age. I knew enough parents of teenagers to realize it wasn't going to last forever—those days where they come home from school and spill their guts to you instead of going straight to their rooms. I knew she'd be popular when she grew, and that she'd soon want to hang out with her friends instead of me. So, really, the fact I could see her at all now was something to cherish. We were on borrowed time.

I went to Target and bought out the kids' section: balls, toy guns, board games, everything. Then I went to pick her up at my old home. Jen herself greeted me at the door.

Every conversation we had had recently was about the logistics of divorce or childcare, but I ventured to ask her about herself.

"How have you been doing? I mean, really?"

I could tell she was trying to hold back a smile. "I've been doing okay. Busy as always. How about you?"

Mia appeared in the doorway, then ran up to me and wrapped around my leg.

"Daddy! You're here!"

"I'm here! Where do you want to go for Dad and Mia's date night?" I asked.

"What's a date?"

"That's when we bring somebody who we love to do fun things."

"Oh. I want every night to be a date night!"

"So, what do you want to do?"

"Pizza!"

"That's not something to do, that's something to eat!"

"Claw machine!"

"Ha, you crazy. Round Table it is."

Jen and I waved goodbye, and I set off with Mia to the Round Table Pizza near the freeway. While we ate, she excitedly told me about her classes and her sports. We played the claw machine, and I had Mia practice the Spanish from her classes by talking with the guy at the register. *"Hola,"* she said, so excited and so loud. "Como estas, y tu?"

"Mia, they're supposed to ask you, *'Y tu!'*"

The guy laughed. Mia was infectious, that white-blonde hair making her look like an angel.

After dinner, we went back home. I had all the toys prepared for a night of crazy fun, but instead we just got in my bed. I put on a Disney movie — Frozen — and she curled up against me, her hand rising and falling with my chest. She fell asleep in a blanket-wrapped taco. I muted the movie and listened to her quiet breathing. *This* was what I had been missing all these years, those quiet moments where I could just feel the life I had created.

Every Tuesday and Thursday night after that, Round Table was on the menu for dinner before our sleepover. In the year and a half that I lived in that apartment, she never once used the spare room. We would lie in my bed and talk for hours.

We started a tradition to play a game called Rose, Thorn, Bud. Right before she'd go to sleep, I'd ask Mia for the best part of her day, the worst part of the day, and what she's looking forward to tomorrow — rose, thorn, and bud.

She'd sit there with her hand on her face thinking for a few seconds.

"I've got a lot of roses!" she said once.

"You've got to just pick one," I said.

"Well, hanging out with you is my rose. But can I also say that I won my soccer match today?"

I looked at her and smiled. "You say hanging out with me is your rose every time. You can just say your soccer game, and we'll assume hanging out is another rose for both of us."

"Okay, well that's my rose! What's yours?"

"Hanging out with you," I said, waiting to see her childlike need for the rules to arise. I loved when she crinkled her nose.

"You did what I just did."

"I did? Oh, shoot, you're right! Okay, my rose was closing a big, big deal at work today."

She rolled her eyes. "Ugh, boring." Then she laughed.

It was everything. It was exactly what I had lost after my cancer, when I could barely muster the energy to get out of bed and be there with her. It was the only time that I felt really complete, like all the shit I went through was all worth it. I had lost everything but could crawl back out of the darkness and regain the best thing to ever happen to me.

* * *

Tuesdays and Thursdays were the best nights. But when I didn't have Mia, I still had to face the discomfort of living alone and forging a new path for myself in sobriety. More than anything, I needed to settle into a routine to keep my mind occupied and stay out of making mistakes. I had to reintroduce myself to the people who had gotten to know the out-of-control me, the guy who could guzzle two bottles of wine without a stomach.

I knew I had to get into the routine of smiling and stopping to chat when I saw my neighbors, of heading downtown and stopping by the cafe, of going into the office instead of working from home, no matter how forced it all felt. Just like they told us at AA, I had to make a routine out of not drinking. I no longer had the *go, go, go, harder, bigger* mindset that had pulled me through my whole life, leaving a wake of destruction behind me. Now it was one day at a time.

When I would head to downtown Tiburon, I could tell people were looking at me differently. Former neighbors seemed to greet me a little less warmly, sticking around for fewer bits of conversation than usual. It made me feel distant from the town I thought I had come to know so well. I made up for it by calling my friends from earlier in my life several times a week. I wanted to reconnect and make up for the years I spent without them.

Several of those friends recommended that I get back into the dating scene.

"Go out, don't fight the fun," was the way Rick, a friend from college, put it.

"I don't know. I've got this thing going with Tanya."

"But she's in Southern California, right?"

"Yeah. I've been down to visit a couple of times in the past few months."

"Come on, man. You're coming off a divorce. Don't hitch yourself to someone you can only see once a month."

I saw the sense in what he said. Besides that, I wasn't always entirely sure what Tanya's intentions were. When I was interacting with her, she never gave me the impression that we weren't heading in a good direction. But still, I was a little jaded by my marriage.

I followed Rick's advice and set up a Match.com account. I quickly matched with a pretty brunette who lived in San Rafael and had a daughter around the same age as Mia. *Good start.*

We met for dinner at an Italian place. We were having a good time, making get-to-know-you small talk about—what else—our kids.

"Mia's getting into all these sports. I feel like I don't have time to hang out with her when she's bone-tired after a day of school, soccer and softball."

She was smiling. "Oh, yeah, mine's like that, too. They seem to schedule something every day. I like it though, keeps her busy during the week."

The server brought out a tiramisu for dessert and we ate it together. When we were halfway done, though, her expression changed.

"I just wanted you to know, if this goes any further, my daughter always comes first for me. *Always.* Then my work comes second, and then third is my man. It's always going to be in that order."

"Okay, sure—"

"But I want my man to put me as number one, always."

"Uh, okay."

"And if you're not going to do that, I can tell you it's not going to work out."

"Well, all right."

Then we got quiet, and I tried to save the conversation by changing the subject. But it was different, and we left each other outside the restaurant with an awkward hug.

Why the hell would someone ask me to put them before my daughter, especially if they weren't going to do the same? Tanya never asked me to do that. Tanya never asked me to do anything I didn't want.

*What am I doing?* I thought. *I've already wasted so much of my life, and now I'm just going to waste more of it on first dates that I don't even care about? I've already got the person who I need. None of this other stuff is going to make me happy.*

This whole time, I had been approaching relationships all wrong. I had always been looking for someone who fit some kind of profile—*Is she attractive? Does she want to have kids? Is she successful and ambitious?*—and if they did, I thought we could be together. When Jennifer and I met, she checked the majority of the boxes, and so I felt that we were a good match. But, of course, just because you think you're a match doesn't mean it's best.

With Tanya, I knew I felt it. She was always there to listen to me without any judgment. She provided a safe outlet for me to honestly talk about my struggles with alcohol. I had spent thirty years putting on the persona of a wild, fun, partying Steve who never said no, and with her, luckily, I could drop my guard and go back to that high school kid who she knew decades earlier. I could leave my adult persona, and my baggage, at the door and decide exactly what I wanted to be. So why was I trying to sabotage my feelings over some hypothetical concern about her intentions?

After the date, I called Tanya.

"I just wanted to say, even though I know we both have so much going on, I really think I want to be with you. I want to make this work."

"That's so great to hear. I want to make this work, too. But why are you saying this now?"

"I — I went out on a date. And it was just, not bad, but just not what I wanted. I'm just tired of being uncomfortable."

"I know what you mean. You're changing a lot in your life, and you've got a lot to discover about yourself."

"You make me comfortable. I want to be with you."

"I want to be with you, too. I just wish we were closer."

\* \* \*

In late December, I had my first chance to put my new, sober self to the test. I got an invitation to the Goldbergs' annual Christmas party.

Adam and Julie Goldberg, the type of picturesque couple who just seemed like they woke up in a fitted suit and an evening dress, lived near our house at the top of the hill, and they invited Jen and me to the party every year. By this point they, and the rest of our local friends, all knew we were divorced, but I think they didn't want to deal with the awkwardness of inviting only one of us, so we both got invitations. We both, of course, accepted, not wanting to be the one who didn't accept.

The party was held at their Spanish-style home, complete with valet service. I had heard through the grapevine that Jennifer would be bringing her new boyfriend, a younger Swedish guy named Christopher who I had met a few times around town in previous years. He drove a Ferrari, and to me seemed like a younger, flashier version of myself. I wasn't jealous, though. When I first heard Jennifer was dating him, it made me feel oddly happy. As much as it would hurt to see her with someone else, I was glad she was moving on from our divorce and all of the pain she had been feeling.

I wanted desperately for Tanya to be able to come with me, but we agreed that we needed to keep our budding relationship under wraps until my divorce was finalized. Jen would always think of Tanya as the mistress, and I didn't want anything to jeopardize the shaky, cordial relationship we had established as we continued to divide up our property.

I walked alone up the hill to the party, smoking a cigarette and trying but failing to come up with a convincing excuse to turn back around. Eventually, I made myself a deal. I'd stay for an hour, just to show people that I was back and that I could be sober and still go to events. Then I'd go home and treat myself to some ice cream.

After a short pause outside, I walked into the party and greeted the hosts, who were both holding glasses of wine.

"Glad to see you back out, Steve," Adam said.

"Wouldn't miss this for anything," I replied. The mood felt strange, like the conversation died as soon as I walked in. Like people had been talking about me before I walked in the door. Of course, it was all in my head.

"Would you like a drink?" he asked, then recoiled when his wife nudged him with her elbow. "We have some sparkling waters at the bar."

"Sounds refreshing."

They gave a modest chuckle and quickly excused themselves to go talk to other guests. The place was already filling up, but Jen hadn't arrived yet.

I didn't feel the energy yet to go up and have a conversation with a random person, so I walked over to the bartender and got a glass of ice water, then sat down on the couch next to a spread of cheese and sushi and desserts. Eating felt like the most socially acceptable alternative to drinking while at a party. Right as I was spreading some pate on a cracker, the hot new couple walked in the front door, and the hosts beamed from across the room and greeted them with a noticeably loud, "Ohhh, Jennifer!"

Jen and her boyfriend quickly made the rounds of the party, drawing laughs and smiles from everyone they passed.

I stood from the couch as they walked up to me, and her boyfriend Christopher reached out his hand. "Good to see you, Steve."

I wiped my hand on my pant leg. "Good to see you, too," I said, my mouth half full.

We stood there for a second, wobbling on our feet, until Jennifer gave a lippy smile. "Don't forget, you're picking Mia up at the academy tomorrow, not school."

"Oh, got it. Sounds good."

Then she turned around, and they walked away. I sat back down and resumed stuffing my face.

My stomach—or lack of a stomach—gurgled as people laughed and talked around me. I started to make myself sick, sitting there, eating sashimi alone, but I didn't know what else to do. I felt small sitting on that couch.

Then I thought back to the time when I was sick, to how much worse it made me feel to hide my thin frame under huge sweaters, to hole myself up so people couldn't see how bad I looked. I thought of how liberating it was that day at Blackie's Pasture to just go up and tell that woman my story—to put all my cards on the table.

Then I realized how ridiculous this all was. Why was I hiding from the people at this party? It wasn't helping anything.

I stood up and went over to a neighbor who was between conversations. He had a kid who was the same year as Mia at school. I hadn't seen him in over a year.

"Steve! What have you been up to?"

*Just put it out there. None of this matters.*

"Oh, man, I've been all over the place. I'm sober now. I just got my own apartment, and now I'm here at my first party with my now ex-wife over there with her new boyfriend. It's pretty awkward!"

*Okay, maybe that was a little aggressive.*

He took a breath in and stopped for a second, holding it. "Oh. Wow. Well, shit, you're nothing if not a survivor. I know you'll make it through." He shifted on his feet. "Well, it's good to have you out here again. We've missed you, buddy." Then he laughed, gave me a pat on the shoulder, and excused himself.

It was weird, undeniably, but I also felt a huge weight come off my shoulders. What did I have to lose? This was my story, my life, and people could either accept it or not.

*None of this matters.*

The rest of the party was awkward, with an elephant clearly in the room as Jennifer and I passed each other a couple dozen times in the house. But it was fine. One way or another, I'd be able to leave here and go sleep in my bed.

As the clock wound down on my commitment to stay there an hour, I just thought of Tanya as I leaned against a wall sipping my sparking water.

I left right at 9 p.m., only saying goodbye to the people I passed on the way to the door and called Tanya right when I got outside.

"How was it?" she asked.

"It didn't actually go as bad as I thought. I mean, it was definitely weird, and I wished you could've been there with me. But I was fine. I didn't die, and I didn't drink."

"Well, I'm proud of you."

"I think I'm realizing that I can't ever give up some of those fun experiences from my past. I still want to be around people who are drinking. I want to do what my friends want to do, and I don't want them to be uncomfortable around me. I still want to go to bars. I want to have fun. I just don't want to drink."

She was silent for a few seconds. "I think as long as you stay committed to the things you need to do, you can be in whatever situation you want. Maybe we can make you an alter-ego. The new Steve is 'Steve the Ex-Partier.'"

I thought about it. *Steve the Ex-Partier.* I liked it. I could say to people: *You don't want me to drink. I did a lifetime of drinking in twenty-seven years, and now the world has cut me off.* I didn't have to hide. I could embrace it.

"Steve the Ex-Partier. I like that."

# CHAPTER

# TWENTY

I did a lot of reflecting about my life as I lived alone in my apartment surrounded by the cackling of the wine-guzzling old ladies and the *arff*-ing of their tiny dogs. Cases and cases of wine were strewn everywhere in my apartment as Jen and I finalized our divorce and divided up our possessions. But the wine just didn't tempt me anymore. I had lost so much before, and there was no way I was ever going to risk it again.

I came to the conclusion that, over the previous five years, I had fallen short in three realms of my life: being a man, a husband and a father.

I wasn't a man because I hadn't acted mature. I had burned bridges while chasing something I was never going to catch. I had told friends who said they were concerned about me to go screw themselves. I had thrown budding friendships in Tiburon in the trash, ashamed of what people in this small town would think of how far I had fallen.

I worked to mend those bridges, reaching out to my old friends and new friends alike. I wanted people to trust me again, and I wanted them to believe me when I said I was better. Still, I could now accept that it would just take time and repeated, continuous effort.

I hadn't been a father because I couldn't care for Mia, and ultimately because I lost majority custody in the divorce. But I thought I was making up for that now. I was never once late to pick her up on a Tuesday or Thursday, and I happily shepherded her to the dozen extracurriculars she did.

And then when I didn't have Mia, all I had to achieve were the don'ts—don't drink, don't do drugs, don't fuck up.

Last, I hadn't been a husband because I could never give Jen security that I was here for her and for our family. I wasn't a team player, and it destroyed us.

I wanted a second chance to be a good husband. Tanya and I came out into the open with our relationship in May 2014. We started talking about moving in together, but first we wanted to make sure Mia would get along with Tanya's son, Kai. So, we all took a vacation to the beach in Southern California with our kids. Could we form a family out of thin air?

At first, everyone there was skeptical of each other, as if we had convened them for a reality show and then told them the twist: *This is your new family!* But Tanya and I tried to keep everything relaxed, to take some of the pressure off. The kids laughed and body surfed together, and we got along with the ease of a happy family.

With all of these things in my life coming together, I wanted to explore one more realm that I had largely avoided all these years. The thing that went way back to the source: my biological parents. I started working on a plan with my half-brothers to get my two biological parents to meet for the first time in more than 40 years.

* * *

The plan coincided so perfectly with the time I was at in my life—a time of rediscovery, of stripping everything away down to its bare essentials, of remembering where I came from instead of the person I had become. And a time of new possibility. I wanted Mia to come with me on the trip to meet her technical grandparents, and Jen allowed it to happen despite a healthy amount of skepticism.

Ron and Penny lived just an hour apart from each other in Minnesota by this time. When I had approached Penny with the plan, she was supportive—she would basically do anything for me at this point to make up for her decision to give me up for adoption all those years ago. The only hitch would be Ron, who given the chance, would almost certainly say no.

We invented a story that we were hoping to meet up with the rest of Ron's family. Then, once Ron picked Mia and I up at the airport, we'd spring the surprise on him. I hoped that he, a recovering alcoholic like me, would see this as his chance to fulfill Step Nine—to make amends. Lord knew he had never done it before then.

Ron and his son, Ron Jr., who was in on the plan, picked us up and drove us south from Minneapolis. There wasn't any snow falling, and a plow had cleared the highway earlier that morning, making it an easy drive in the zero degree weather. The car was silent, with Ron sitting in the passenger seat, his hands on his knees, and Ron Jr. driving. The flat white landscape did nothing to distract me from the thoughts racing through my head. Penny was ready, and she would need me to text her soon.

We sat in the car for a long time as I wondered when would be the best time to ask the taciturn man in the front seat to do just one thing for me in my life.

*What am I hoping to get out of this? Do I want them to both hug me from either side at the same time, like on a TV show?*

It took a flight to Minnesota for me to realize I wasn't really sure what I wanted out of this. I guess I just wanted to make something happen that never would have happened before. If the cancer or the drugs or the booze had killed me, they never would have seen each other again. But since I was alive, I could make something happen out of thin air. I felt a surge of confidence, and I finally spoke up when we were about an hour and a half outside of Duluth.

"Ron," I said. "I have a favor to ask you."

He inhaled sharply and grabbed his knees.

"The answer is no, Steven. I'm not going to do it."

It caught me off guard. Did someone tip him off? I took a few seconds to gather myself.

"Ron, I've never asked anything from you my entire life. This is the one opportunity for you to sit down with Penny and me. I'll never ask you to do anything again if you just do that for me."

"I won't do it." He said it without moving his body or looking at me, and the car fell silent for a long time as the wheels continued to roll past the snowy fields.

I stared at him, silent and stone-like, and wondered how I, a person who fills every space possible by talking, shared genes with this man. Mia squirmed in her seat, looking bored and anxious. Ron Jr. gripped the wheel with both hands.

After several billboards screaming *YOUR AD HERE* rolled past us, Ron finally broke the silence.

"Fine. I'll do this one thing for you, Steven. But we're going to do it in a public place, and it's only going to be thirty minutes. And that's it. Period."

I was shocked, and I rushed at the opportunity. "Fine. Done. Where should we meet?"

"We'll meet at the McDonald's in Esko."

I almost laughed. One of the most momentous occasions in my life, at a McDonald's. "Okay, great."

I pulled out my phone and quickly texted Penny. *It's on. McDonald's in Esko. We're an hour out.*

Once we got to the tiny town, Ron Jr. took Mia to an arcade nearby to meet with two other half-brothers who lived in town. Ron and I pulled up to the McDonald's and walked in the jingly door.

My fourth half-brother, Erik, followed us in and took a table near the entrance like a secret service agent. Sitting at a far corner of the restaurant in a booth was Penny, fidgeting with her hands. We passed up the register, ignoring the confused expression on the cashier's face, and walked up to Penny's table.

Ron sat in the booth opposite Penny, and I sat on the end of the table between both of them. I gave her a hug in the booth.

"It's good to see you again, Penny."

"It's good to see you too, Steven."

Everyone was quiet for a few seconds.

"Last time I saw you was 1971," Penny said gently to Ron, breaking the silence.

"No, I saw you at the courthouse in 1972," Ron said. "You tricked me into thinking I was signing food stamps when it was actually some adoption paperwork."

"That ... never happened." Her voice quivered.

"You told me my son had died."

"As if you were ever going to come to help us to begin with." She was teary. "You made it pretty damn clear you were never going to be there for us."

They argued back and forth for several minutes. Was I supposed to be upset they were arguing? I wasn't, weirdly. I felt at peace. I had put the chess pieces in place, and whatever happened after that was up to the players. The fact that this meeting happened at all was amazing.

They argued for a while, venting years of pent-up resentment, of real and imagined injustices. Then, in that miracle of unspoken human forgiveness that I had the pleasure of experiencing so many times in my life, their voices started to quiet, and they talked a little bit about their families.

Finally, he paused, and his face softened a little bit. "Any mistakes I've made in the past, I'm sorry for. I was too young and scared to—"

*Beep-beep, beep-beep, beep-beep.*

Ron stopped mid-sentence. I looked to see where the noise was coming from. He looked down to his wrist and hit a button on his digital watch. Then he stood up and put on his coat. "Thirty minutes. We're done here."

I was mildly shocked, but I held my tongue. Literally thirty minutes on the dot. *My god, this man.* But, you know what, it was fine. He did exactly what he said he would.

"Thank you both so much for doing this," I said. "I really do appreciate it."

Then, just as Ron said, it was over. He walked out the door. I lingered behind to talk with Penny a little bit. Then we said goodbye, too, and I walked with Ron over to the arcade, where my half-brothers were playing at the batting cages with Mia.

"Steve, how'd it go?" Ron Jr. asked me.

"It went ... as well as I could've ever imagined."

We decided to take turns on the fastest pitching machine. My four half-brothers went before me. One after another, they whiffed on the pitch, missing it by a second or more. As I went up to the plate and faced the machine, though, I knew I could do it. I swung at the first pitch and hit a ball off to the side. Would've been a foul in the MLB, but here it might as well have been a home run. The guys whooped behind me. I felt proud of what I did, of what I could do.

Later that night, Mia and I headed to the airport to get on a red-eye home. When we boarded our flight, she was fidgety. Everyone else on the plane was quiet, and Mia spoke to me in almost a whisper.

"Daddy, can I ask you a question?"

"Of course."

"Are you and mommy going to be like Ron and Aunt Penny?"

"You can call her Grandma Penny, Mia."

"She's grandma?"

I thought for a second. "Yes, she is."

"Oh. Are you and mommy going to be like Ron and Grandma Penny?

"What do you mean, sweetie? Are you asking if we're not going to see each other at all?"

She nodded tentatively, looking like she might start crying.

I put my hand on her bleach blond head and pulled her under my shoulder. "We aren't going to be like that. We've made some mistakes, but we care too much about you, about our family, to let what happened to Grandpa Ron and Grandma Penny happen to us. We'll always both be there for you. Mommy will. Daddy will. And mommy and daddy will, together."

I saw the worry melt away behind her eyes, and she nuzzled her head into my shoulder and quietly fell asleep.

# EPILOGUE

In early 2019, when I was thinking about how to end this memoir, I imagined the cliché movie scene where the hero sails off into the sunset, a content half-smile spread across his face, and a voiceover tells the satisfied audience, "Lessons were learned, and he died decades later on an island somewhere off the coast of Fiji."

At that time, more than 10 years after I first felt that stomach pain in China, it really felt like my life was behind me, like I was now suspended in some sort of afterlife where problems didn't weigh on me as heavily. After all the dips and rises of my journey, everything had leveled off. The highs weren't as high anymore, but the lows weren't nearly as low, either. I was, in short, the happiest I had been, surrounded by the people I loved.

I was living with Tanya and her son, Kai, along with Mia for half of every week, While the custody arrangement technically remained the same, Jen allowed me more and more time with Mia as I proved I was a changed person.

We rented a new house in an enclave of Tiburon called Paradise Cay. To get there, you have to drive on a two-lane road on the windy western side of the peninsula, then nosedive down a steep hill before arriving at a neighborhood with dredged-up roads that extend into the bay like fingers. The streets were wide and quiet, giving the kids a place to play without worry.

I thought often of the home I lived in with my parents on the tranquil little street in Saratoga, how much a particular place could evoke a sense of safety for a kid whose biological parents had given him up. I hoped that I could give the same security to both Mia and Kai.

Tanya and I waited another year after coming out publicly with our relationship in the summer of 2014 before driving a U-Haul full of her stuff from Orange County up to Tiburon. When she came up, I felt totally whole, like everything I wanted was within my grasp. I proposed to Tanya the next year with the kids watching on our back deck.

As we planned our wedding, the circle of what was just supposed to be close friends and family in attendance, of course kept widening until the whole thing was a source of stress instead of fun.

One day in December, about five months before our wedding date, Tanya was pacing around the house after meeting with her mom and dad about it. Suddenly, she got an idea.

"Let's just do it at City Hall," she said. "Why do we need to be all extravagant?"

"Are you serious?"

"Yeah, why not? What does it matter anyway? We've both already had big weddings."

"Music to my ears."

That made me love her even more. None of that showy stuff was for us. We just wanted to do something with the most important people.

The next month, Tanya's parents, my biological mom, and my best friends—Rick, Tom, Buddy, Aaron—all came to San Francisco. I hired the limo driver, Bijan, to come drive us around the city from the wedding lunch at Absinthe to San Francisco City Hall.

For the wedding, we had the option of picking the thousand-dollar rotunda on the top level or the hundred-dollar lower level, which had just a stand and an altar. We were fully invested in doing this wedding as simply and cheaply as possible, so we picked the lower level. We met with a judge who didn't look a day over ninety years old, signed our paperwork, and then waited outside the chapel behind several other wedding groups for the quick ceremony.

Suddenly a roar echoed in the airy chambers of City Hall. We all turned our heads. It took half a minute before we saw what was making the noise. A dancing group with a full drumline was celebrating Brazil's Carnival. They ran through the main lobby, shouting as they kicked high in the air to the continued *boom, boom* of the massive skin drums.

The judge couldn't talk above the din. He walked the line of waiting couples up to the top floor rotunda to get away from the noise. Even there, it echoed over the walls, and the first couple had to yell their vows into each other's ears. We laughed about it, but I was already thinking of how to get my hundred dollars back.

Then, right as Tanya and I walked up with our party, the music suddenly stopped. It was like the clouds had parted, revealing blue sky. I was standing in front of the most beautiful woman I'd ever seen, the woman who I had been with so many years ago, and with whom two decades apart felt like nothing. Mia and my best friends surrounded us — the most important people in my life. This was exactly where I wanted to be. I didn't want the moment to end. Our spoken vows echoed off the walls, repeating themselves in our ears. I kissed her, and we embraced. It probably all took about five minutes in total, but I still remember every second of those five minutes.

As we left down the massive staircase, the band resumed playing in the lobby, and we danced our way out to the limousine.

Our reception was on our back deck. A few dozen of our friends and family, along with our kids, spent hours back there talking and dancing. I felt so loved, and it was all so simple and beautiful and caring. Right then, I could tell how far I had come. The kids were happy, my friends were congratulating us. There was no big wedding, but our relationship was never about the big wedding. It was always about embracing the fact that every moment was here, *here,* and there's no other way it could have been.

After the wedding, much of my life became about the kids. I was Mia's Uber driver to soccer and basketball practice every night, with In-N-Out burgers in between. Just as I had thought earlier, the preteen years brought out some distance for Mia. I showered her with (probably too much) affection and gratitude, telling her in the car how lucky I was to see her when I picked her up from school.

"I could've missed all of this! I love you, and I'll always love you," I'd say, to eye rolls in response.

At night, I'd go into her room and ask her for a minute of her time. She would often say, "Okay, whatever," then set her phone timer for sixty seconds.

"Really? That's all I get? I'll remember that for when you need something." But I was kidding—I remembered what it was like at that age.

I didn't feel any regret or anger when Mia wanted to spend more time in her room or with her friends than she did with me.

I'd still always remember that I got a hell of a five-year run out of it. And I cherished that time even more by seeing how bad it could have gone, how I could have missed all of that had I kept making mistakes. And if I had died from the cancer, she never would have remembered me at all. All she would've had to remember her dad were pictures. We got to spend more time than I ever could have dreamed of together.

So now, even if something goes wrong in the future, at least she'll have memories of date night at Round Table, where we'd hold hands across the table. Or of our walks along the bayside park where I'd pass a soccer ball to her. Or of the time I taught her how to ride a bike and she picked it up like she'd been on two wheels her whole life.

I could tell Kai started looking up to me as the model for a father. And I worked to make him feel as close to my biological son as I could, even if it meant sometimes siding with him over Mia. I remembered the feeling of not knowing if you're really loved or accepted, so I worked hard to make him feel like this home was his home, too.

It was painful to me when I got the cancer that I'd never be able to have a kid again, so Kai coming into my life and becoming close to me was like a miracle: I got the son I never thought I'd have.

Besides my family, I delved into other things to keep me inspired every day. A few years ago, I came across an organization called Debbie's Dream Foundation, which is a nonprofit devoted to stomach cancer. What first got me involved in the organization was their lobbying work in Washington, D.C., where they attempted to get money allocated toward gastric cancer research. Since I started doing that work, we've gotten millions of dollars per year allocated towards stomach cancer, and in the last year that amount increased to over eight million.

However, the truly inspirational part of that organization for me has been the mentorship work they do. When I was going through my cancer, I didn't really have anyone to talk with about what I was going through. The only person I had was P.J. Gallaway. But instead of being a bright light who illuminated the room for me, he was only a point of light just in front of me. When he died and that light went out, I was lost in the dark, trying to navigate it all on my own.

Now I spend hours every week helping people through various stages of diagnosis, surgery, and recovery from this cancer. Doing the mentorship work, I've been told by several people that my story gave them inspiration to keep pushing for another day, another hour. It's fuel to me, and it has kept me from making any more mistakes. It's the AA model: after one person gets sober, they become a sponsor to help other people on that same journey. The mentor's responsibility for the other holds them accountable in their own life, and the chain continues.

\* \* \*

Because of all that, it felt right that I should end this story sailing off into the sunset without a worry in the world. But of course, just because you sail off into the distance doesn't mean you won't hit choppy waters on the open ocean. And my life didn't stop just because I decided to write a memoir.

At the beginning of 2019, on almost the exact anniversary of my surgery eleven years earlier, I was in Los Angeles on a rainy February day with Tanya for our one-year anniversary. We were lazily browsing paintings at the Getty Museum. We had been there about an hour too long, and every other breath was a yawn. Suddenly, while we were standing in a room of abstract paintings, I felt a sharp acid pain in my abdomen. I groaned and sat down.

"What's wrong?" Tanya asked, a worried look already on her face.

"Maybe just a little acid reflux," I said, trying to remain calm, to keep to my mind away from the instant recollection of what happened on the Great Wall of China. I tried to stand, but a nauseous feeling traveled up my stomach and into my throat, so I sat back down.

Tanya sat next to me and asked a flurry of questions: "Are you okay? What are you feeling?"

"I'll be okay. I'll be okay. It's alright, I've felt this before." I was lying, sort of; I hadn't felt a pain like this since I had cancer.

"Okay. Okay. I guess you know your body better than anyone."

It eventually settled enough for us to go to dinner that night, but then restarted with a vengeance right when I got my entree. We had to leave the restaurant before we could finish our meal.

We flew back the next morning and Tanya immediately took me to Marin General Hospital. The doctors drew my blood and poked and prodded me, and then I sat and waited while they tried to figure out what was wrong. The pain felt like someone was reaching inside of me and squeezing my organs. They kept me overnight, and then again for another night.

Finally, after days of doctors entering the room and telling me in a million different ways that they didn't know what was wrong with me, they decided to transfer me to Stanford. Marin General wasn't equipped to deal with someone who had my medical history.

*It's back. It's back. It's fucking back and this time there'll be nothing we can do about it.*

I couldn't believe it was all happening again, almost exactly the same way it started before. The staff at Stanford stuffed me behind a curtain that fit just my bed and a single chair. It blocked me from seeing other patients, but it didn't block me from hearing their moaning throughout the day. And I myself was in such agony that I'm sure I added to the chorus. Along with my new bed came my dear old friend the little green button—the Dilaudid drip to control the pain. The nurse started to give me an explanation of how to use the button, but I stopped her. I knew how this worked. The little pain controller fit so comfortably in my hand, and I scared the shit out of myself with how quickly I pushed that button when it lit up every fifteen minutes.

My déjà vu got even stronger when I ran into Christine, the nurse who originally called the Code Blue when I was going into sepsis ten years ago. I asked if she remembered me.

"Of course, I remember you! I've never done anything like that since then."

"Neither have I!"

She looked excited to see me. Clearly this incident had left a mark on her. Then her eyes drifted down to my hospital gown, and she seemed to snap out of it. A sad look crossed her face. "I've got to go do my rounds," she said.

We hugged goodbye.

As I lay in that bed, waiting for the doctors to figure out what was going on, I became convinced it was the worst-case scenario. Everything that I worked for in the past decade was out the door. If the cancer really was back, I would just take all the pain pills I needed to numb the pain and die. *I won't go through chemotherapy again*, I thought during the times I sat alone in bed.

But then when Mia, Kai or Tanya came in, I regretted those thoughts. I had a new family. How could I just give up on them?

Could I even write this memoir? Could I tell people an inspirational story about how they can conquer anything in their lives if I'm still just as susceptible to those self-destructive cycles as I had been a decade earlier? How could I tell other people how to live their lives if I couldn't even live my own?

Finally, on my second day at Stanford, the doctors came back with the best news of my life. It wasn't cancer. It was my gallbladder.

I barely had a chance to breathe a sigh of relief before the doctor spoke again. "We have to remove it immediately."

"Remove my gall bladder?"

"Yes."

"What does that mean? Can I live without that? I'm already down like, three organs."

"Yes, you can live without it. But we need to do it right now. It has gangrened, and it could rupture and kill you."

He gave me a form to sign and, suddenly, four orderlies appeared and wheeled me to an operating room. The surgeon injected me with Propofol and gave me those familiar directions: *Count down from ten.*

I stayed in the hospital for about four days. At one point, I woke up screaming in pain, with Tanya, Mia and Kai all around me. Mia couldn't bear to see it and had to rush out of the room while Kai held my hand and comforted me before a doctor gave me an injection that knocked me out.

I sported a new scar across the whole front of my abdomen, forming a sort of X with the older scar. I tried to put on a strong face for Tanya and the kids and friends who called, but after a couple of days, I just couldn't do it anymore. I pointed my phone at my face and recorded a video to post on my Facebook.

"I've had a brutal morning so far, but I'm making progress."

I pointed the camera down at the first breakfast I'd gotten to eat in several days—eggs and hash browns and coffee. "In the big picture, as bad as I am, this is nothing compared to what I've been through and what other people are going through. This is painful now, but it's easy compared to what I've seen in the hospital. I should not complain at all, but I'm gonna complain a little because today sucks."

\* \* \*

My last day in the hospital, Sharon—an old friend from junior high who I use to walk home from school with—came to visit me. She brought these colorful streamers that could tie around your head, we put them on, and she said we were going to parade around the hospital. We walked up and down the hallways playing the song "Celebrate" while people who looked sick and dying smiled at us all along the way.

I was again sent home with a prescription for OxyContin to manage the pain. However, in the decade since I had gotten my stomach taken out, doctors had significantly wised up to this pill's addictiveness, so they only prescribed me twenty milligrams per day, with a strict limit on getting refills. It was like taking sugar pills compared with my peak of more than four hundred mgs per day. Still, I gave the pills to Tanya to regulate how much I was taking every day.

As I lurked around the house with my head in that familiar haze, I worried again whether I would be able to get off these pills once my prescription ran out. I barely ate, and within two weeks, I weighed one hundred eight pounds. *Is this happening again?*

No. This time was different. The last time, when I would try to start weaning myself off the pills, I would go into a deep dip of pain and depression that seemed endless. But what made the dip that much worse was that I couldn't see where the pain ended. This time around, even though I couldn't *feel* what it was like on the other side, I knew there was a better place all the same. I knew I just had to get myself up out of bed and walk around, to get my body moving and keep my mind occupied.

And I had a wife who was supremely patient and supportive this time, too. To be fair, Jennifer's experience was harder and much more drawn out, but I got a taste of how Tanya would react to hardship. She understood that I had to take the pills, and that just because I was taking them didn't mean I didn't want to get off them. I was scared, but she helped me keep the confidence that I could really come out on the other side of this.

Slowly, every day, I was able to walk farther, to take one less pill, to eat one more bite. One weekend day, I had been on the couch the whole morning when I started to feel down on myself. Tanya was sitting next to me, watching the news.

"Will you just walk with me to the club and back?" I asked. I felt kind of pathetic asking it—the club was only two blocks away.

"Of course," she said, without a bit of hesitation in her voice.

I put on pants and a hoodie, and we set off down the sidewalk. The wind was blowing strong against us, and I had to lean my body forward to fight it. I felt like I might fall over. But I kept pushing, and finally after several minutes of slow walking, we made it to the club. I was exhausted, but we walked back, and I collapsed onto the couch. It was always the small steps that got me back to living the life I wanted. That would be as true now as it ever was in the past.

From the time I got sick up until a few years ago, I had experienced life as a series of problems. Anything that got in my way or was unexpected was a problem—another hitch stopping me from living the life I was supposed to live. But thinking that way only pulled me further into negativity, because life was just never going to work out exactly the way I wanted it to.

This time around, I tried to look at my issues as challenges, not problems. A challenge necessitates commitment to overcoming it. A problem is something to avoid or to get around. I had already spent too much time in my life avoiding my issues.

This time around, too, I had more than just my family to keep my feet to the fire in honoring my commitments.

\* \* \*

In my mentorship work with Debbie's Dream Foundation, I've been working with one man, Gunner, who got diagnosed with stomach cancer in 2019. Like so many, he went straight to the Internet and read all the horror stories of this cancer. That's always a mistake—all it did was stress him out, and the last thing his body needed at that time was stress.

Gunner, who lives in Minnesota, reaches out almost every day with a host of questions—Should I avoid this food? How many pain pills can I take? Is it normal to not poop for a week?—and I've tried to answer every question he has with my own honest experience.

I had never met Gunner until recently while attending an Advocacy day on Capitol Hill in Washington DC, but he still feels like someone I know. He shares everything with me, and I try to give him my honest experience while imparting some hope for the future. He has said that I have given him more hope in any fifteen minutes of our conversations than he had ever gotten in his life. He told me, "I don't ever say this to anyone, but you are my hero."

It makes me uncomfortable to hear from people that I'm a hero. I'm not entirely sure what I've done to be called that. In some ways, all I've done is survive. But at the same time, I try to temper my ego and tell myself that the reason they think of me that way is because they need someone to look up to, something to look forward to.

So, given that's the way he feels about me, how could I not try to live up to be that person he puts on a pedestal? It tore me up when P.J. died. I couldn't do that to Gunner.

So when I was sitting at home in that familiar drug-induced haze after my surgery, I thought often of those people I'd mentored—some of them still alive, many of them not—and how much of a letdown it would be for them to see me fall from the place I've gotten. It was with their images in my mind that I grimaced through the pain and reduced my OxyContin intake by one pill, two pills, until a few weeks after my surgery, I took my last pill and threw the bottle away.

* * *

Even as I do my work with Debbie's Dream Foundation, I don't delude myself or others with the thought that everyone's going to make it out alive. The survival rate for gastric cancer has gotten better as more patients have had the surgery I did. But the overall statistics are still not great, and I've known a number of people in my work with the foundation who have succumbed after what seemed like a promising start. Debbie Zelman, the founder of the organization, herself died just a few years ago.

After he got his stomach removed, Gunner found he had no complications, and he was going through his post-op treatments smoothly. In all, he felt good. I was staying positive, telling him to keep it up, but I felt I had to be honest with him, too.

"I'm just saying, that's not the experience I had. I came into a lot of roadblocks. So, enjoy what you have right now."

Like clockwork, two weeks later, it all crumbled when he got a blockage. He started coughing up blood. He had to go to the ER once, twice, three times. He got depressed. The crash was even harder because he felt like he was in the clear.

*This is the way it is*, I texted him. *And it could even get worse. I couldn't get out of bed for weeks. But I wouldn't change it because it made me who I am now. You can do it.*

I can never pretend for people that the recovery process won't be difficult. It will. The only thing I can really do is guide them to avoid the worst things I did when I was recovering. I told Gunner again and again about my experience on pain medication, and how bad that got—the only time I ever actually wanted to kill myself was during the withdrawal from OxyContin—and as far as I know, he has been able to stay out of the deep with the meds. Things like that feel like a small victory.

Still, with more than a decade between my life now and my cancer diagnosis, it all starts to feel a little remote. Last November, I went to a gastric cancer symposium, where I met three other survivors. Between the three of them, it had been six years since their diagnoses—only half the time I had survived by myself. Nonetheless, they had twice the passion that I did. They had all the answers, they knew to do this or do that, and how to get over *this* and how much *that* sucked. They were full of fiery optimism, all the while I couldn't help but think, *Oh, my god, things were bad for so much longer than the first year. These guys might not even be out of the weeds yet.*

At a certain point, though, I have to accept that they can fill a role that I can't. While in a sense I do remember the agony of having cancer, I don't exactly remember what the pain was like. It's like trying to remember a dream after being awake for ten hours: The broad contours are still there, but the specifics are harder to conjure. I have to assume the role of an elder statesman: the one who's on a pedestal, where everyone else can hope to someday reach.

But there is one thing I know I can offer to everyone, whether it's cancer survivors, alcoholics, addicts, or anyone else who reads this book. I *know* that you can come out on the other side of any dire situation totally transformed, as long as you have something or someone to keep you inspired to get better.

Back before I got sick, I was living only in the future, thinking about what the next big thing would bring me, where I could get to from here. Then, when I got the big C, the fact that the future only looked bleak tore me down into a complete depression. To counteract that, I wanted to push the envelope, to party harder, to see more new places, to travel more. Then I'd wake up in the morning and wouldn't want to do anything—the life was drained from me.

But there's a right way and a wrong way to live in the moment. After I recovered—*really* recovered—from the cancer, the drugs, and the booze, I found that I wanted to get out of bed again. I wanted to be a part of my daughter's life, to learn more about my new wife, and to be a father to my new stepson. It became about the little things, like riding bikes with Mia down the street. Or just getting up in the morning with Tanya and sitting for a cup of coffee.

Only now do I realize that expression about how *I could get hit by a bus tomorrow* is really more profound than it is a cliché. The truth is, there might be no future other than this day right now, and so I try to live my life accordingly. The only way to do that is to accept what I've done in the past and embrace that as part of myself. That's the only way I can really be free of it. After that, I just have to take control of the things I can control and accept the things I can't.

And I really do take control of everything I can. When I became sober, I had to decide for myself what things in my life I wanted to give up and what I didn't. I didn't want to give up the fun I had hanging out with my friends while we were drinking. But, of course, I did want to give up drinking. Now, with a clear picture of what my goals are in life, I can't even say I feel the temptation to drink. But we still have a hell of a time together.

Much of that comes down to taking control of my own story. My story—the things that have happened to me, the things I've done right, the things I've done horribly wrong—is a part of me. I can't change that. But the times when I've tried to hide it and hide myself are the times I've been brought to my lowest moments. And in those moments, the things I've tried to push down come roaring out anyway.

For some people, maybe that's a worthy trade-off—a sense of stability for the majority of your life, with just a few moments of total explosion. But I could never pull that off. I embrace the identity I've created for myself. I'm Steve the Ex-Partier, the guy who still wants to be part of the fun but who's been cut off from drinking. I wear my story like a shirt, and some people certainly don't like it, but others are refreshed that someone's being honest and react with some honesty about their own lives.

That's ultimately what this story is about, and what I always hope to leave my kids with at the end of the day. Honesty is the only thing that matters, with yourself and with others.

In the end, though, there's one question that still burns at me. How can people get to the place where I am—of accepting your past, living totally in the present with the people you love—without going through what I went through?

And the thing is, I don't think there's an easy answer. I think it either takes a ton of humility, an absence of ego, or an absolutely devastating life event to get to where I am now.

But even if I never get an answer to that question, I think that if my story can provide hope to even one person—make someone think, *Hey, somebody else got out of the shittiest, most awful experience ever, maybe I can do that, too*—I'll consider my mission accomplished in writing this book.

Hell, it could even be the difference between life and death.

Made in the USA
Middletown, DE
27 February 2021